WITHDRAWN

P9-DEN-043

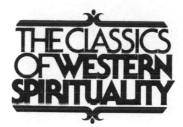

THE CLASSICS
OF WESTERN
SPIRITUALITY

THE CLASSICS OF WESTERN SPIRITUALITY
A Library of the Great Spiritual Masters

President and Publisher
Kevin A. Lynch, C.S.P.

EDITORIAL BOARD

Editor-in-Chief
Richard J. Payne

Editorial Consultant

Ewert H. Cousins—Professor and Director of Spirituality
Graduate Program, Fordham University, Bronx, N.Y.

John E. Booty—Professor of Church History, Episcopal
Divinity School, Cambridge, Mass.

Joseph Dan—Professor of Kaballah in the Department of Jewish
Thought, Hebrew University, Jerusalem, Israel.

Louis Dupré—T.L. Riggs Professor in Philosophy of
Religion, Yale University, New Haven, Conn.

Rozanne Elder—Executive Vice President, Cistercian
Publications, Kalamazoo, Mich.

Mircea Eliade—Professor in the Department of the History of
Religions, University of Chicago, Chicago, Ill.

Anne Fremantle—Teacher, Editor and Writer, New York, N.Y.

Karlfried Froelich—Professor of the History of the Early and
Medieval Church, Princeton Theological Seminary, Princeton, N.J.

Arthur Green—Assistant Professor in the Department of
Religious Thought, University of Pennsylvania, Philadelphia, Pa.

Stanley S. Harakas—Dean of Holy Cross Greek Orthodox
Seminary, Brookline, Mass.

Jean Leclercq—Professor, Institute of Spirituality and
Institute of Religious Psychology, Gregorian University, Rome, Italy.

Miguel León–Portilla—Professor Mesoamerican Cultures
and Languages, National University of Mexico, University City,
Mexico.

George A. Maloney, S.J. — Director, John XXIII
Ecumenical Center, Fordham University, Bronx, N.Y.

Bernard McGinn — Associate Professor of Historical
Theology and History of Christianity, University of Chicago
Divinity School, Chicago, Ill.

John Meyendorff — Professor of Church History, Fordham
University, Bronx, N.Y., and Professor of Patristics and Church
History, St. Vladimir's Seminary, Tuckahoe, N.Y.

Seyyed Hossein Nasr — President, Imperial Iranian
Academy of Philosophy, Teheran, Iran.

Heiko A. Oberman — Director, Institute fuer
Spaetmittelalter und Reformation, Universitaet Tuebingen, West
Germany.

Alfonso Ortiz — Professor of Anthropology, University of
New Mexico, Albuquerque, N. Mex.; Fellow, The Center for
Advanced Study, Stanford, Calif.

Raimundo Panikkar — Professor, Department of Religious
Studies, University of California at Santa Barbara, Calif.

Fazlar Rahman — Professor of Islamic Thought, Department
of Near Eastern Languages and Civilization, University of
Chicago, Chicago, Ill.

Annemarie B. Schimmel — Professor of Hindu Muslim Culture,
Harvard University, Cambridge, Mass.

Sandra M. Schneiders — Assistant Professor of New
Testament Studies and Spirituality, Jesuit School of Theology,
Berkeley, Calif.

Huston Smith — Thomas J. Watson Professor of Religion,
Adjunct Professor of Philosophy, Syracuse University, Syracuse, N.Y.

John R. Sommerfeldt — President, University of
Dallas, Irving, Texas.

David Steindl-Rast — Monk of Mount Savior Monastery,
Pine City, N.Y.

William C. Sturtevant — General Editor, Handbook of North
American Indians, Smithsonian Institution, Washington, D.C.

David Tracy — Professor of Theology, University of Chicago
Divinity School, Chicago, Ill.

Victor Turner — William B. Kenan Professor in
Anthropology, The Center for Advanced Study, University of
Virginia, Charlottesville, Va.

Kallistos Ware — Fellow of Pembroke College, Oxford;
Spalding Lecturer in Eastern Orthodox Studies, Oxford
University, England.

The Theologia Germanica of Martin Luther

TRANSLATION, INTRODUCTION AND COMMENTARY
BY
BENGT HOFFMAN

PREFACE
BY
BENGT HÄGGLUND

PAULIST PRESS
NEW YORK • RAMSEY • TORONTO

Cardinal Beran Library
St. Mary's Seminary
9845 Memorial Drive
Houston, Texas 77024

2-20-96

54743

Cover Art
LIAM ROBERTS was born in Ireland and now lives in New York. After attending the
National College of Art in Dublin for five years, he studied at the Academy of Fine
Arts in Florence, at the Royal Academy of San Fernando in Madrid, and at the Academy of Fine Arts in Rome for one year each on scholarship. The cover art is a composite
work bringing together a contemporary reproduction of the well-known portrait of
Luther entitled "Luther in der Predigermütze 1528" by Lukas Cranach, Luther's coat of arms (said by some experts to be of kabbalistic origin), and a few lines
from the original edition of the *Theologia Germanica.*

Design: Barbini, Pesce & Noble, Inc.

Copyright © 1980 by
The Missionary Society of St. Paul
the Apostle in the State of New York

All rights reserved. No part of this book may be reproduced or transmitted in any form
or by any means, electronic or mechanical including photocopying, recording or by
any information storage and retrieval system without permission in writing from the
publisher.

Library of Congress
Catalog Card Number: 80-50155

ISBN: 0-8091-2291-X (paper)
       0-8091-0308-7 (cloth)

Published by Paulist Press
Editorial Office: 1865 Broadway, New York, N.Y. 10023
Business Office: 545 Island Road, Ramsey, N.J. 07446

Printed and bound in the
United States of America

Contents

Cardinal Beran Library
St. Mary's Seminary
9845 Memorial Drive
Houston, Texas 77024

Editor of this Volume

Bengt R. Hoffman is a native of Sweden and received his basic philosophical and theological education there. He has served as priest and rector in Church of Sweden parishes. He earned his Ph.D. at Yale University, specializing in Christian systematic and ethical thought. Since 1967 he has been professor of ethics and ecumenics at the Lutheran Theological Seminary at Gettysburg, Pa. He is the co-author and author of numerous books and articles in Swedish. His books in English are *Christian Social Thought in India 1947–1962* and *Luther and the Mystics.* He is a contributor to *The Journal of Ecumenical Studies, The Lutheran Quarterly,* and other periodicals.

Dr. Hoffman has spent altogether a decade in ecumenical posts in Geneva, Switzerland, as secretary for work among refugee students and Christian high school movements in the World Student Christian Federation, as leader for the World Council of Churches' post-war inter-church aid in East and West Germany and Austria, as chairman of the Ecumenical Team Committee of the W.C.C., and as Director of the Department of World Service of the Lutheran World Federation. He has traveled all over the world in his ecumenical tasks. Until the Chinese revolution he spent two years as a missionary among students in Shanghai, China. His ecumenical work began during World War II when he served in the Prisoners of War Aid of the World's Y.M.C.A. in England, Canada and the U.S.A.

Dr. Hoffman is a member of several learned societies, two of them by election: Pro Fide et Christianismo and the Nathan Söderblom Society. He is included in the work, *Contemporary Authors.* In addition to his offerings on theological and contemporary ethics, in his teaching he examines the relation between mystical theology and the moral life in Luther's thought and treats of Christian outreach in the third world. He co-teaches a course on Aquinas and Luther with a Roman Catholic colleague from Washington, D.C.

Dr. Hoffman has a D.D. from Wartburg Theological Seminary. He is married to Pearl Willemssen, a librarian and senior high school teacher in French. They have two daughters, both of them teachers.

Author of the Preface

Bengt Hägglund is professor of systematic theology and symbolism at the University of Lund, Sweden. He earned his doctorate at the same university in 1951 and has been attached to its theological faculty since that year. He is one of the major authors on Reformation and post-Reformation thinking including the mystical thought of the late Middle Ages. Some of his writings are: *Theologie und Philosophie bei Luther und en der occamistischen Tradition* (1950), *De Homine* (1959), *History of Theology* (1968), "Luther und die Mystik" in *Kirche, Mystik, Heiligung und das Natürliche bei Luther* (1967), *The Background of Luther's Doctrine of Justification in Late Medieval Theology* (1971), and "Renaissance and Reformation" in *Luther and the Dawn of the Modern Era* (1974).

Preface

According to this medieval tract a fundamental distinction must be made between the world of creation and the eternal, spiritual world. This should not be understood only as a metaphysical presupposition but also as a challenge to man to accommodate his life to its eternal destination and not to live as if this earthly life were the only one.

Therefore the anonymous author takes us into an inner dialogue, where he not only informs the reader about the truth he has found about God and man, but also invites him to apply the eternal rules in his own mode of life, the rules laid down in the human mind and revealed in the prophetic wisdom of the Bible and in the life of Jesus Christ, the only one who has in a perfect way brought together time and eternity, earth and heaven, the eternal, spiritual reality and an earthly, human life.

The author knows not only the three renowned stages of mystical experience: purification, illumination and union (ch 12), that we usually combine with a special kind of introspection and self-training; he also knows what he calls "the two roads in his heart," that is the experience of hell and heaven in the true contrition over sin and the awakening of a new, spiritual life.

Only when a man comes to know himself and feels his unworthiness and the condemnation brought upon him through his skin, can he be led to the situation where he "does not ask for anything but the eternal Good alone and knows that the eternal Good is exceedingly precious" (ch 11).

What is here described as hell and heaven in the human mind, as the two roads in the heart of man, is a parallel to what Martin Luther and the other reformers did teach in other terms in their doctrine of penance, of contrition and faith, awakened in the conversion of man through the effective divine word, through the law and the gospel.

There is *one* mighty hindrance for everybody to lead a good life in a right relation to God and to his neighbor, i.e. in a true love. The name of this fundamental evil is "I" and "mine" and "me." If anyone is to reach his true destination and find his right place in his earthly existence, he must deny himself and give the glory to God. "My many words on the subject"—says the author—"can be summed up by a few: Cut off your self, cleanly and utterly" (ch 20).

As the editor has pointed out in his commentary, this does not mean "an obliteration of self but rather a reduction to nothingness of 'I-dom' and 'self-dom,' the self-centered ego of our temporal existence, the 'lower self' " (fn 146 below).

The exhortations to "relinquish the things of the world," to turn away from the manifold and partial interests and seek the eternal and perfect Good does not, in the context of this tract, mean a denying of life in its usual, worldly conditions. The true Christian is anxious to live according to the orders of life in his personal existence, wherever it may be. And the temporal world belongs to God, who is everywhere and at the same time above all. "There is nothing without God except one thing: to will otherwise than the eternal will" (ch 42).

PREFACE

To restore man to the state of obedience to God and bring him to overcome the self-serving egoism is the central concern towards which all the thoughts of this book converge. "It is a great folly for man to imagine that he can do anything by himself" (ch 42). God is all in all and therefore the man has to deny himself, i.e. not "ascribe anything good to oneself since goodness only belongs to the true Good" (table of contents, 2).

For the author this wisdom is a common truth, so clearly founded in the Reality itself, the reality about God and man, that if no one had hitherto expressed it, it should be necessary to find it out and verbalize it. But it coincides with the revealed truth of the Christian faith. What he says about the two ways of life, the false light and the true light, the false love and the true love, he finds likewise revealed in the Bible, for example when the apostle Paul speaks about the old man and the new man, the first Adam and the life of Christ, or when Jesus Christ himself exhorts his disciples to deny themselves and follow him (Matthew 16:24; ch 17).

The two modes of life are sharply and uncompromisingly described, as the contrasts of disobedience and obedience, of false love and true love. Behind the one stands Lucifer and behind the other Christ. The transition from disobedience to obedience is not a separate occurrence provoked by the human will, but rather a continuous process, into which the follower of Christ is drawn, in the true contrition and under the guidance of the Spirit. The new life is described as a gift received in the sacrament (ch 43). This is a way where "he comes into possession of the eternal Good," a way to peace, joy, ecstasy, delight, a "foretaste of heaven in this present time" (ch 11).

The *Theologia Germanica* belongs to the living tradition of Christian mystics. Its strange history through the editions of Martin Luther and Johann Arndt and so many other editions in different languages shows that it retains an abiding value, not only as a historical testimony from an influential stream of medieval thought, but also as a useful guide to a deeper understanding of Christian faith and the foundations of a Christian mode of life.

The language of the tract is simple and straightforward. Martin Luther speaks in his preface of 1518 about its "unembroidered and ungarlanded words" and asks the reader not to become irritated with its style. For a modern reader these qualities seem to be more an advantage than a shortcoming, even if the style is much more concentrated than we are used to in modern books.

Bengt Hägglund

Foreword

Theologia Germanica or *Theologia deutsch* is a book about life in God as it translates into life in the world. It was written around 1350 by an anonymous author. Martin Luther came upon a shorter version of the tract in 1516, provided it with a preamble and had it printed in Wittenberg. Two years later he found a more extensive copy of the work in a monastic library, probably the original rendering in toto. He published it, in 1518, with a slightly more elaborate introduction.

Many editions appeared in Luther's life-time. The total number of editions through the centuries, in different languages, amounts to about two hundred.

The book was written in an orthographically inconsistent vernacular German. Its language is "simple", says Luther. But this, he adds, should deter no one for the spiritual guidance offered is indeed profound. Also, it is now happily available in ordinary German parlance.

As far as is known, none of the original manuscripts exist today. The basis for English translations or transpositions into modern German is a manuscript of 1497. It was long considered more faithful to the original than the Luther editions. However, later scholarship accords to Luther's offering the greater authenticity. This is to say,

Luther very likely made no alterations before handing over the mystical-ethical work to the printer.

The present translation has been entitled *The Theologia Germanica of Martin Luther* since it is based on the Reformer's "edition" of 1518.

Luther wrote that, next to the Bible and St. Augustine, he had never read anything about God's way with man, as helpful and true as this little book. It confirmed his experience of being justified by grace. His kinship with the unknown author and with Johann Tauler, as well as with some other mystics of the late Middle Ages, suggests a union in the Body of Christ, transcending ecclesial boundaries, through *sapientia experimentalis*, the heart's knowledge of Christ's presence here and now.

Theologia Germanica is close to the teachings of the Friends of God, groups for renewal of spiritual and moral life in the 14th and 15th century. It addresses itself not least to the ethically questionable "liberation" movement called the Brothers and Sisters of the Free Spirit.

The book is therefore no flight from existence—as popular notions of the mystical life in God will have it. It is rather a guide to true rest in God for the sake of true moral responsibility in the affairs of men.

Across the centuries the anonymous spiritual leader in *Theologia Germanica*, here introduced by Martin Luther, brings us a message just as timely now as in the 14th and 15th century.

In fifty-six brief chapters it describes the soul's relationship to Christ; the wiles of the devil working through our nature; the obstacles on the road of a seeker: self-will and pride; the process of "divinization" as unredeemed nature is crucified; and the signs of the Christ-life: the liberation from rule and the obligation of rule.

In the Translator's Introduction the historical setting of the book is outlined. Attention is also given to the close inter relationship between Christ's presence and the melting down of one's false pride, on the one hand, and organically ensuing ethical tasks in ordinary life, on the other. A theological and linguistic Commentary as well as Biblical references are attached to the text in a Note section.

Introduction

On the Anonymity of the Book

We have in front of us an anonymous book on life in God. The anonymity is likely to remain even as older manuscripts are gradually uncovered. For anonymity belonged to the style of the author and had become a survival issue for him.

It belonged to his style as a Christian. He believes that God "speaks the book" through him.[1] That is the same kind of boasting Luther has in mind when he says in his Preface that he will speak as a fool. Not to advertise one's name is one way to let God come to the fore. It is foolishness in a sense but, deep down, what difference does it make if an errand is carried out with the name of the dispatcher attached? After all, the errand is what counts.

But anonymity may also have been a matter of physical survival. The established church did not always look with favor on the movements for personal renewal that arose in the late Middle Ages. We know from the lives of some of the mystical teachers that they were under surveillance, suspected of heretical teachings—heretical in the sense that they did not readily conform to the demands of institutional fealty and scholastic, rational purity.

1

Thus, as Luther points out in his 1516 Preface, only God knows who wrote the book. Luther read the introductory information with the same lack of specific information as we have. The author belonged to the Teutonic Order and apparently spent a goodly part of his lifetime at its center in Frankfurt am Main, as "a priest and a warden." After the Crusades and activities in Jerusalem this order had been remolded into a domestic community of service and evangelism with a dual responsibility: to care for the sick and to do battle against false belief. The order's "uniform" was a white gown and a black cross. The members were divided into knights, priests, and serving brothers. Only German noblemen became knights. The order received many land grants. In the 1300s the gravity of its work shifted from West German cities to East Prussia. It was probably through the Teutonic Order in Prussia that Luther came upon the Small Theologia in 1516.[2]

The reasons why *Theologia Germanica* is generally thought to have been written around the middle of the fourteenth century are several. Most of them have to do with the way in which the book reflects a certain historical situation. We have just discussed the matter of anonymity. In the next section we shall consider the reason why, precisely in the first half of the 1300s, people who embraced thoughts about God and man, as expressed in our *Theologia*, would find it wise to remain unknown to the world.

The Interdict
Part of the background to *Theologia Germanica* is the struggle between the pope and worldly authorities in the beginning of the 1300s, one of the battles between *sacerdotium* and *imperium*.[3]

For our purposes let us enter the historical account at the time of the struggle between two emperors, Fredrick

2

INTRODUCTION

of Austria and Louis of Bavaria. Fredrick was supported by Pope John XXII, for no altruistic reasons, to be sure. The Avignon period in the history of the papacy (1309–1377) rendered the pope so dependent on the French kingdom that attempts to expand papal influence on Teutonic territory became almost a logical outcome. What Louis lacked in papal favor he sought to supplant with support by provincial electors in his empire. He thus had to make the best of a not very enviable position: He had to rule in the tension between the papal claim for absolute sovereignty and the countervailing ambitions of independent states. Because he chose to throw in his lot with the latter he was also willy-nilly drawn into the movement for church reforms. In fact, the question of whether the church should be governed absolutistically or democratically became a live issue during the attempts of worldly rulers to extricate themselves from the administrative bondage under the church.

Fredrick's death in 1322 left Louis the sole ruler of the Germanic realm. Anxious to improve conditions within his empire, he was open to a settlement with the pope. However, Pope John XXII was not about to compromise. He refused to enthrone Louis. The emperor launched military attacks, first against northern Italy and later against the city of Rome. He had himself crowned there and also installed a "parallel" pope.

The gravest outcome of the struggle was the Interdict. According to the Interdict of 1324, Louis and all those who remained loyal to him were excommunicated. Until the middle of the fourteenth century European Christians lived under the shadow of the Interdict.

Emperor Louis encouraged his subjects to pay no attention. The urban laity favored resistance to the pope. The clergy, by and large, sided with the head of the church. The result was that in places where lay people were on the emperor's side years went by without much ecclesiastic ministry. Public worship came to a halt. Only baptismal services and the rite of extreme unction took place.

A decade and a half into this Interdict period an imperial manifesto, buttressed by various princes, defended the emperor's claims, rejected papal accusations against Louis, declared him rightfully chosen by the electors, and accused of treason each and every one who did not accept the message. Disobedient communities and individuals would lose their civil rights.

The manifesto was an open declaration of all-out defiance. It probably met with a great deal of approval among the public. Such was the general climate with respect to the church in the waning Middle Ages. But in many instances the emperor's action tended to exacerbate the situation. In Strasbourg, for instance, Dominicans and Franciscans, loyalists in the imperial cause, had for years said mass despite the threat of papal excommunication. But the emperor's manifesto demanded of them too overt a defiance of the curia. They discontinued their services and were promptly expelled by the magistrate.

Under the cloud of a dual banishment many clerics and monks became perennial exiles on the European continent. Some of them were known to earn a living from hearing confession. Others, less mercenary, became assets to the revival groups who called themselves "The Friends of God" and about whom a word will be said a little later. In some cities, some priests chose not to buck worldly orders; for varying reasons they stayed on with their charges performing holy rites despite the wrath of Avignon.

By and large confidence in ecclesiastical hierarchy and order was on the wane. Renaissance humanism had caused part of the erosion. But growing materialism and worldliness among priests and monks and in institutional structures certainly contributed to the disillusionment. Spiritual yearning frequently and more readily found expression through channels other than churchly establishments.

The tapestry against which the background of *Theologia Germanica* has to be seen also contained calamities of a more physical kind. The first half of the 1300s was troubled by earthquakes, violent windstorms, and the ravages of the plague. From the life story of Johann Tauler we know, for instance, that his practical work of mercy was carried out among people dying from Black Death.

Perhaps we can say that Renaissance man, as the fourteenth century wore on, began to discover the frailty of his optimism. He began to lose his faith in assured progress. If Renaissance man was also touched at all by the church's teaching of God's providence he would tend to look at major catastrophies as divine judgments. Much unredeemed superstition came to the fore in attempts to ward off further misfortune. One was all too prepared to read catastrophies as signs of the impending Latter Day. People expected the second coming of the much revered Fredrick II, the thirteenth-century emperor. He would bring social justice and take to task the corrupt in state and church. Chronicles from the outgoing Middle Ages sometimes depict for us the peace marches of those times: bands of repentant folk traversing southern Europe in display of their contrition, with the task of warning against continued ungodliness, and in the hope that intense and loud prayers on their part and true penance on the part of all would avert further evil.

The scapegoat mechanism in the human psyche was also triggered. The Jews became its target. The Jews by their very existence offered an irresistible opportunity to blame it all on somebody else. This flight from reality seems to occur especially in times of grave misfortune. The burning of Jews by frightened so-called Christians in the fourteenth century provides us with another of the many examples of how people may praise the Lord with their lips while their hearts are far from him. It should be of no comfort whatever that burning feared folk was a fairly common solution to problems during the era in which our devotional *opusculum* took shape. Prior to the Interdict, Philip, king of France, compelled the pope to abandon his protection of the French Templars whose landed property the king coveted. In the process he had monastic knights burned at the stake in Paris, including the vicar general. The burning of Jews was an even deeper confession of fear masquerading as purification of faith.

The Interdict unleashed forces that laid bare unresolved spiritual problems. It illustrated how tenuous was the unity culture under the sponsorship of the church. The uncertainties of man's life became more apparent. More and more people were looking for signs and experiences of the eternal life that, especially according to the Gospel of John, is available here and now, and *in* a person, not only *outside* of him.

The Friends of God

In the midst of the turmoil of the late Middle Ages and as a reaction against it, a quiet revival of the spiritual life took place.[4] The "practice of the presence of God" led many to the discovery that God is indeed not far from any of us. In order to cope with the vicissitudes of life man may, in quiet contemplation, draw strength and love from a higher world. Eternal life, engendering inner peace, is here and now. This was the spiritual rediscovery of thousands. The theological term for experience of divine presence is *sapientia experimentalis*. Martin Luther used that term as part of what "justification" is.

The discoveries were made by small groups meeting for devotion and discussion in different parts of the European continent, from the Netherlands to Italy and Hungary. Although the association between the local groups was not administratively tight or formal, people in the movement maintained contact with each other. As we have seen, some traveling priests and monks were involved. And letters went back and forth with mutual information and encouragement. Cologne, Strasbourg, and Bale soon became centers for this twelfth-, thirteenth-, and fourteenth-century revival of contemplative, mystical theology. Many of the leaders belonged to the Dominican monastic community.

Most of the fourteenth-century participants in the mystical renewal described themselves as "The Friends of God" (*Gottesfreunde*). The name was derived from John 15:15: "No longer do I call you servants, for the servant does not know what his master is doing; but I have called you friends, for all that I have heard from my Father I have made known to you."

The Friends of God taught renunciation of self, the ongoing revelation of God through the work of the Holy Spirit in man, and the ultimate union between God and man. They rejected religion based on fear or promise of reward. They were decidedly opposed to the libertinistic, antinomian, and antichurch ideas of The Brothers and Sisters of the Free Spirit. *Theologia Germanica* was in large part written to counteract the influence of the so-called Free Spirits. We shall return to a brief consideration of the people and the ideology thus connoted.

The Friends of God believed that, before God, laity and clergy are on equal footing. For the sake of Christian discipline the organization of the church was considered essential.

As there was no fundamental distinction between

clergy and laity so there was no discrimination with respect to sex. Some of the leaders were women. The con-
vents of Engeltal by Augsburg and Maria-Medingen
near Nuremburg, for instance, seem to have served as
movement centers. Letters written by the Ebner sisters,
mother superiors of the two institutions, are filled with
spiritual counsel in the Friends of God tradition.

The reader of *Theologia Germanica* will find numerous
indirect references to this international, medieval community of experiential Christian wisdom. Already the brief
introduction to the book and its anonymous author actually employs the expression that must have served as a
password and an open sesame: "God has spoken this little
book through . . . a friend of his."

The Friends of God preferred unobtrusiveness not
because they were antiecclesial, for most of them were decidedly not, but because they did speak about an inner
way that seemed to threaten the positivistic ceremonial-
ism of the church. As a consequence they placed much
value on spiritual communion between like-minded souls.
Many were the letters, books, recipes, medicaments, and
white handkerchiefs with the name of Jesus embroidered
in red that went from community to community. Meister
Eckhart advised his listeners to receive well those "godly
persons" who could open their hearts only when they
came across like-minded souls. That nation is indeed
blessed, he said, which has many of them. No doubt he
had the Friends in mind.

A modicum of secrecy was, of course, also prompted
by the sometimes precarious relationship between throne
and altar, as was said above.

*   *   *

INTRODUCTION

Among those medieval mystics whom Martin Luther cherished most were the Frankfurter, author of *Theologia Germanica*, and Johann Tauler of Strasbourg. Indirectly Tauler plays an important part in the *Theologia*.

Tauler was a Dominican monk and priest who preached the gospel in the towns along the Rhine up to his death in 1361. When the Interdict of 1324 had come into force, Tauler wrote an appeal to the clergy exhorting them not to abandon their charges. If the emperor had committed wrongs against the church, he said, who was to be blamed but the emperor? Why should his subjects suffer from that?

Tauler followed his own advice. During the darkest days of the Black Death this fourteenth-century mystic stayed behind in Strasbourg rendering practical and spiritual assistance to the sick and dying.

Nicholas of Strasbourg was a close soul mate of Tauler's. A study of his sermons makes it plain that he must have been part of the secret brother- and sisterhood out of which *Theologia Germanica* grew. He was born in Strasbourg and in time became one of the leaders at the monastery in Cologne and finally overseer or nuncio for all the Dominican centers in the German lands.

We should note at this point that the movement called The Friends of God was by no means coterminous with proconciliarism or proimperium. Some Friends, like Nicholas, just mentioned, remained loyal to the Holy See. This is also true of two other remarkable Friends, Heinrich of Nördlingen and Heinrich Suso (Seuse). Both of them were banished for their loyalty to the pope. Heinrich of Nördlingen corresponded with Christina Ebner in the Dominican nunnery at Engeltal and with Margareta Ebner at the nunnery of Maria Medingen. In one of his letters he wrote: "Pray for our dear father Tauler; he is constantly in great sorrow because he teaches the truth as whole-heartedly as any teacher I know." The background was of course "the jeering" from those who rejected Tauler's warnings. Heinrich of Nördlingen has been described as a "secular priest."

Heinrich Suso, a native of the country around Lake Constance, was eighteen when he entered the Dominican friary at Constance as a novice. After some time of strict obedience to the monastic rules he had a conversion experience. "I was," he said, "by a sudden change released from the chain." After that he saw more clearly and more painfully the frivolous and empty life of the friars. He reacted against their laxity. For a decade he devoted himself to the most excruciating schedule of mortification. When his health became gravely impaired he was told in a vision to abandon this kind of corporal punishment. He threw his neck girdle, his undergarment with leather straps and iron nails, his spike-studded leather gloves, and the wooden cross with protruding nails into a river. At the age of forty Suso renounced asceticism entirely and became an itinerant preacher and a part of the Friends movement. He was all the more free to travel as the city council of Constance in 1339 had ordered that church services must be resumed, in accordance with the imperial edict. Suso, like some other Dominicans, decided to observe the papal Interdict. They were subsequently ostracized from Constance.

Tauler became a father confessor for many among The Friends of God. One of those was Rulmann Merswin of Strasbourg. He belonged to a prominent family and had led, as he says, an unchaste and worldly life. He and his wife decided to abandon the business circles in which they moved and join the free association, The Friends of God. Tauler became Merswin's father confessor.

Merswin bought an old monastery, Grüner Wörth, near Strasbourg, which he thought of as a spiritual retreat

center and for which he became the virtual leader although it was later formally owned by the Knights of St.
John. Merswin left a legacy of devotional works and mir-
acle stories the origin and historical veracity of which are
uncertain. He claimed that some tracts in his possession
were written by "a layman, A Great Friend of God."
Some have suggested that this friend "from the Ober-
land" was Nicholas of Bale. The experts are divided on
the question. A book supposed to deal with Tauler's life,
the *Meisterbuch*, has been the object of much discussion. In
fact, some scholars, Denifle in particular, have come to
the conclusion that the layman Merswin, in his desire to
underline the legitimacy of Christian lay leadership in a
clerical age, himself wrote the literature he ascribes to a
mythical Friend of God. This anonymous Friend of God
who according to Merswin's literary legacy has exerted a
very great influence all over the continent was, it has been
argued, Nicholas of Bale, a layman who after many years
of itinerant spiritual counseling was burned in Vienna at
the behest of the church. Perhaps the "layman," the
"Great Friend of God," should be considered Merswin's
alter ego and not at all Nicholas of Bale. As noted, Denifle, a Catholic scholar, declared that Rulmann Merswin
hoodwinked everyone. Merswin himself "is the author of
all the writings about the 'Friend of God,'" says Denifle.
On the other hand, K. Schmidt and Preger, Protestant
scholars, asserted that Tauler had indeed written the
Tauler biography that was found at Grüner Wörth
among Merswin's manuscripts. Although this discussion
was carried out in the nineteenth century, the scholarship
of the twentieth century around the truth of Merswin's
claims has not come closer to a solution. I have drawn attention to it here for two reasons. First, numerous accounts of Tauler's life include the story about his
conversion by the mysterious "Layman from Oberwald."

It is, however, by no means certain that we here deal with historical facts. Second, if Rulmann Merswin was a somewhat plausible person, yet a true friend of Tauler and the Friends, we have before us a salutary bit of realism in the midst of what sometimes tends to look almost too spot free, a hagiography of sweet *Gottesfreunde* without visible deficiencies. In authenticated Tauler writings there certainly is a recognition of man's constant tendency to be curved in on himself. And, as the reader will soon discover, *Theologia Germanica's* author shares the insight.

*   *   *

If some figures in Merswin's gallery of Friends do not belong to our determinate existence, the free association of spiritual kin called The Friends of God certainly did.

Of course, the word *friends* was already used in days before Christ to describe those who lived in a particularly intense awareness of God's guidance, presence, and judgment. For instance, Abraham is referred to as a friend of God. And, as we have seen, Jesus considers true followers friends. The martyrs were regarded as special friends of God by Clement of Alexandria and Chrysostom. Thomas Aquinas, in his discussion of the nature of friendship, suggests that the content of the word ultimately derives its meaning from the relationship between man and God.

But in the fourteenth century the term assumed sharper outlines. The reason can only be the appearance of "free thinking," a humanistic-secular kind of argumentation about religious and existential matters. *Theologia Germanica* is much exercised about it. As already announced, a brief separate treatment will therefore be accorded those persons in late medieval times who considered themselves to be of a "free spirit." Perhaps mainly due to Tauler's influence—much in evidence in *Theologia Germanica*—the spiritual battle lines were drawn so that one began to speak of true friends of God and false friends of God. The false ones, the illegitimate ones, were the Free Spirits. This is to say, we are here actually dealing with technical terms connoting different spiritual-theological approaches to revelation and redemption.

The true Friends of God had, we said, no intention of forming a new sect. From that point of view they were indeed no threat to the Roman church. Yet, we have observed that there were tensions between the church and the spiritual cells in question. The explanation is not only the power struggle between pope and emperor. The church was jealous of her prerogatives as the administrator of grace and felt threatened by some of the noninstitutional language in the sermons and the writings of the Friends. It is possible that the Friends who belonged to the radical Beguines or Beghards contributed to the anxiety of the established hierarchy. Be that as it may, the *Theologia Germanica*—and therefore indirectly, one might suppose, the Friends—was the object of Catholic disapproval especially after Castellio's Latin translation appeared in 1557. The pope banned the work officially in 1612, rejecting all versions of the book "printed in whatever idiom." One list of forbidden material alludes to the *Theologia* as "a most unhealthy book." The Roman Index of 1948 limits its censure to Castellio's work of translation. It should probably be regarded as significant that Roman Catholic scholar Joseph Bernhart chose the Würzburg edition as his text, " despite its imprecisions."[5] One could assume that this did not happen in complete ignorance of the official stance of the church. Würzburg probably appeared more faithful to traditional theology than the Luther text, apart from the assumption that it was more original. In most libraries we find translations of

Würzburg rather than translations based on the Luther text.[6]

The "Mystical" Theology of Theologia Germanica

Since *Theologia Germanica* undoubtedly emerged from the Friends movement of the fourteenth century and is evidently close to Johann Tauler, some remarks may be in order about distinctions to be made between various forms of medieval mystical theology and then, especially, about Tauler's views as compared with those of his major mentor, Meister Eckhart.[7]

Since *Theologia Germanica* belongs to the devotional literature that can be classified as "mystical" in the same sense in which Martin Luther spoke of experience of justification as a *sapientia experimentalis*, it is essential to state at the outset that mystical theology or mysticism is not of one and the same kind. It has been fairly common in Western theological reflection since Harnack and Ritschl to assume that mysticism is always the same, in other words, from a Protestant point of view, heretical. It would carry the matter too far to go into this question in the present context except to point out that Luther's obvious lifelong interest in spiritual kin who could be termed "mystical" refutes the generalization that mysticism is always the same, namely heretical.[8]

We have an illustration of this point in the similarities and differences that prevail between Tauler and Eckhart. A few remarks around the subjects *man, God,* and *Christ* will illustrate what unites and separates the two fourteenth-century leaders.

There is something in man that forever unites him with God. The "ground of being" is the locus where God communicates Himself, discloses Himself. Of course, it cannot be realized outside and without Christ. But the fact remains, according to Eckhart, that something in man eternally reminds him that he is meant for God. God "has made man's soul after Himself," the soul is a temple, not yet readied for God's arrival but there; God has created it and He desires that it should be "cleared" for His arrival.[9] Similarly, Tauler maintains that from the "indwelling" of God in man even heathen people know "that God is the creator and ruler of the world."[10] When thoughts of this kind turn up in *Theologia Germanica*, its first modern editor, Martin Luther, had no difficulty reconciling them with his discovery of man's inveterate sinfulness. Both awareness of sinfulness and experience of potentiality in and affinity with God are parts of salvation, in Luther's view. Man is born with a faculty that reminds him that he stems from God. That part within him makes it possible for him "to understand and love the invisible things."[11] But, again, with Tauler and Eckhart and with Luther, it is Christ who does the work of bringing to life within men that which is potentially of God.

Tauler also seems to say the same as Eckhart concerning the Godhead, which is beyond God. The Being beyond all being is beyond human designations. Good and evil, knowledge and love, are not words applicable to the ultimate Truth. "Nothing" is a term for the Godhead. It is shocking to our traditional ways of thinking when Eckhart declares: "In God there is neither goodness, nor better, nor best and he who would claim that God [in this ultimate sense] is good would do God just as great an injustice as a person who describes the sun as black."[12]

In the same manner Tauler speaks of God who "is above order, being, good . . . this or that particular thing." God is "the Godhead above all names."[13] To both Eckhart and Tauler participation in God is in part an experience of the Nought, the Being who is nothing of "this or that," who is not to be confused with the plurality of this world. To experience something of this God-behind-God is to go through a desert, listen to the silence, stand by or fall into an abyss. Mystical language sometimes refers to this experience as "the dark night of the soul." *Theologia Germanica* has the same manner of treating the reality of our world of manifold things counterposed to a God who is beyond names. Luther's description of the "hidden God" similarly reflects the awesome experience of the numinous. I for one believe that his book *The Bondage of the Will* and his way of dealing with the question of predestination in that work give an illustration of the theological intuition that speaks of that face of God which is turned away from us.[14]

But, of course, neither Tauler nor Eckhart limits himself to the negative side of what can be said about God. God has come to us in Christ. And Christ is to them an example challenging man to discipleship, to lead "the Christ life," as *Theologia Germanica* expresses it. But Christ is also a sacrament. He is cosmic power infusing true knowledge, true discernment and love. For in the last analysis the union with God is not man's doing, it is God's deed in man. Luther's Christological thought makes a similar distinction between the historical Christ and the mystical Christ, between *exemplum* and *sacramentum*.

Both Tauler and Eckhart conceive of man-in-God as a being whose deepest ground has been stirred by Christ and who is now becoming *vergottet*, "Godlike," or, if you please, "divinized." The person that emerges from life in God is "the noble person." The nobility does not come about by man's own efforts, only by surrender of self-will. The Godlike or divinized being leads the Christ life because Christ has been permitted to take over the will. Such a person becomes detached from the creatureliness of his existence. That is to say, his attachment to things of time and space eases up. Things of time and space have meaning only before God, the originator and activator.

A divinized person also renounces images as instruments of piety. All images should finally be wrought up in that which is without form, the Godhead.

The third renunciation has to do with the will. The will as seeker of self must go through the experience of inner poverty. This means a complete turnabout, a radical conversion. To let God come into the soul in this manner, to clear the ground for God, is the ultimate meaning of obedience, painful for the lower self yet leading to peace and *Gelassenheit*, inner serenity and peace.

Johann Tauler, who apparently has contributed much inspiration to "the Frankfurter," author of *Theologia Germanica*, shares views of the above order with other leaders among The Friends of God. However, there are points at which Tauler and Eckhart differ. When *Theologia Germanica* commendingly quotes Tauler the verdict does not automatically include Eckhart. Nor should we assume that Martin Luther, by approving of the *Theologia*, thereby indirectly propounded or approved of certain basic Eckhartian ideas.

In one sense Tauler agrees with Eckhart when the latter says: "The eye by which I see God is the same eye with which God sees me. My eye and God's eye are one eye and one seeing and one knowing and one feeling." But he agrees while implicitly disagreeing. For he does not constantly let the natural interweave with the spiritual. Tauler experienced man as a being who will have to make do with the natural as it exists in contrast to the spiritual. There is more of the paradox of human existence in Tauler than in Eckhart. If one simply adds God to nature one is actually dealing with nature all the same. The person who "knows God" does not know anything different from the one who knows nature. But he knows differently. In other words, the Godhead or God can never entirely merge with the world of time and space. For Tauler no added knowledge can bring man to God. The whole secret lies in trusting in the path onto which God leads man. There is a tendency in scholastic reflection to assume that we shall know the final goal by the faculties of our spirit. We find a great deal of Thomas Aquinas in Meister Eckhart on that score. But Tauler and, in general, The Friends of God are rather antischolastic in this regard. They said that we can of course know that which we have garnered of insight and experience in the natural world but the continuation from there on can only be lived. The truth is not coequal with what we shall eventually derive from nature, however deeply we delve. The truth is a paradoxical symbiosis of that which exists in nature and that which does not exist there. Tauler had a tremendous experience of this fact when, as a famous preacher in Strasbourg, he was converted by the mysterious Great Friend of God, a layman. Now, as was said above, scholars do not agree as to whether or not this Friend should be considered historical. Although I tend to side with those who maintain that there is a historical nucleus to the story, let us suppose that the wise Friend was a fictional hero. Yet, that conversion has all the signs of authenticity. For what happened to Tauler was that he discovered with crushing clarity that he had *thought* all the right things about God with his intellect but the thought did not *live*, did not reverberate, had not been experienced within himself. Tauler was transformed from a thinker about the nature of God into a reborn being, a new character, one who lived in the Spirit. He had come to the cross where all values are turned inside out. He had edified his listeners. Now he moved them. It may well be that the story about the forty people that fell down as if dead on hearing him preach after his rebirth is only symbolical. It is good enough as a symbol. For it shows us what The Friends of God had begun to see: that Covenant, Kingdom, or Justification come to life only in the utter reduction of human claims at the foot of the cross.[15]

We can point to another difference between Tauler and Eckhart, the great soul whom he might have met in person in Cologne but in any event had come to know through the written word. I refer to the question of dualism between God and man. In Eckhart's theology the emphasis falls on the Incarnation. For Tauler the cross and the Resurrection are at the center. Eckhart's mystical theology is accordingly inclined toward philosophical-Neoplatonic speculation about the Divine. Tauler speaks a much more pastoral, church-oriented, existential language.

One can discern this with special clarity by focusing on the expression, common among mystics, "the birth of God in the ground of the soul." What Plotinus called the *centron*, mystical writers transposed in varying ways: "the soul's essence," "Gemüt," "synteresis," "the abode of the spirit," "the light of the spirit," "the innermost source," "the heart of the soul," "the ground." To Tauler, the Frankfurter, and Meister Eckhart such terms connoted the meeting place between God and man. But whereas this place of encounter does not give rise to pantheistic thoughts in Tauler and the Frankfurter, Eckhart's way of depicting the God-man relationship seems to lead to a certain lack of distinction among God, man, and nature.[16] It came easy for Eckhart to say: "The more a thing participates in a common nature, the more it is one with the impartibility of the common nature, the more impartible it is itself. . . . Take right as right and ye take it as God."[17] Tauler, although recognizing man's kinship with God, speaks in more dualistic terms about the great distance between man and God and man's nothingness and sinfulness before God.[18]

The birth of God in the ground of the soul is thus less of a continuum from nature to spirit in Tauler than in Eckhart. Perhaps one can apply here the analytical standards offered by history-of-religion scholar and churchman Nathan Söderblom. He distinguished between "personality-mysticism" and "infinity-mysticism." Personality-mysticism is an experience of God in the midst of life's problems, an experience of the human "I" meeting the divine "Thou." Infinity-mysticism is an experience of the superhuman beyond the vicissitudes of life. Personality-mysticism is trust and forgiveness in this life. Infinity-mysticism is immersion in nature and exercise according to technical patterns. On the one hand we have a relationship to a personal God, on the other a dissolution of the person into the impersonal Beyond.[19]

By this method of distinction Tauler and the Frankfurter belong more readily to the category of personality-mysticism and Meister Eckhart in many ways to nature-mysticism. Martin Luther's theological intuition told him that *Theologia Germanica* and Johann Tauler described the Christian condition in ways germane to the Christian faith. Those ways were the ways of personality-mysticism, the *sapientia experimentalis*, experiential Christian knowledge. And Luther's kinship with Friends of God–thinking endured throughout his life.[20]

The Brothers and Sisters of the Free Spirit

The struggle between pope and emperor must have had a devastating effect on many in the latter part of the Middle Ages. The claims of outward establishment, papal or imperial, were losing their authority. The corollary despair issued, on the one hand, in skeptical materialism and, on the other, in religious speculations far exceeding the boundaries of established theology. If we look for signs of the former, we find them, for instance, in the annual "feast of fools," at which ordinary citizens indulged in pagan revelry, gave voice to deep-seated irreverence of superiors, and flaunted magistrate and church. The student songs of those times reflect a mood that, with a twentieth-century term, could be described as existentialistic. It is a mood that moves between nostalgia and hedonism. Carl Orff's musical compositions *Carmina Burana*, based on some of these poems, have caught the temper of the age. A sign of the latter, wild iconoclasm, is the "liberated ones," The Brothers and Sisters of the Free Spirit. We hear a great deal about them in *Theologia Germanica*. They may in fact be the major reason why the Frankfurter committed his thoughts to paper. Their message had basically the same thrust as the experience and teachings of The Friends of God. But they went to extremes, much in the manner as, a century and a half later, some of Luther's original friends, the Enthusiasts or the Schwärmer, became his adversaries.

The theological parenthood of The Brothers and Sisters of the Free Spirit should probably be sought in the apocalyptic ideas of Joachim of Fiore, Amalric of Bena, and David of Dinant around 1200. These incentives were then combined with the poverty ideal of the Beghards, itinerant mendicants. The thrust was antischolastic and anti-institutional but, as we said, the beginnings testified to the same concerns for true Christianity as those that inspired The Friends of God.

The protest movement in question—which never really assumed firm organizational outlines—was rooted in the conviction that all events, everything inside creation, occur from necessity, namely the necessity implied in the faith that no being can exist on its own.[21] Moreover, all created beings are in God and in that sense we

21

cannot assume the existence of hell, devil, or purgatory. Such things have been invented by the clergy. After all, is not God in all created things? Yet, self-will is a fact and self-will must be broken.[22] The Free Spirits introduced unpalatable food in their regimen toward this end. In removing his self-will man gives room for God in this earthly existence. He does Godlike things in order to praise God, not in order to gain reward. Christ suffered, not so that the threat of eternal damnation might be removed from our lives; he suffered rather as an example of progress in the good. The cross of Christ is of little avail without our willingness to shoulder numerous smaller crosses in His imitation and discipleship. Amalric said— and the Brothers and Sisters believed him—that each devoted soul in this way becomes Christ himself *realiter* and *naturaliter*, taking on His nature in this earthly existence.

However, in their desire to free themselves from the fetters of the church the Free Spirits soon began to teach that "God in the self" actually means that "the self is God." The Gothic mood, symbolized in the pointed church spire, displayed its theological weakness very clearly among the Free Spirits. Gothic man assumed that "the crest of the human spirit" could be manifested as God. Yes, he said, he could truly become God. A person permitted to enter the divine becomes imperturbable.[23] As Christ in His passion did not really suffer, in the same manner a liberated person was a free lord and king over all created beings. He could use everything that pleased him and destroy everything that appeared untoward. This presumptuousness was cloaked in a doctrine of false freedom.[24] The liberated spirit was dependent on no order or law promulgated by the church. Only "the gross," the undeveloped, were subject to traditional moral habits. But "the free" stood above the ordinary dictates of conscience, for the free could no longer be distinguished from God.

INTRODUCTION

The Brothers and Sisters of the Free Spirit saw no relationship between life in God and ethical responsibility. Ethical injunction could not be part of the liberated life since the Godhead is beyond ethical characterizations. Libertinism spread through the ranks and, as it did, the number of participants grew. Workers, smiths, swineherds, all manner of folk, left their hometowns in search of the new kingdom that was so imminent and could be grasped all the more readily by those who were free from the shackles of church and society and had become persuaded that a beggar is *eo ipso* closer to the true dearth or poverty of the spirit. The "kingdom" people had, as far as libertinism goes, become indistinguishable from libertinists in the humanistic Renaissance tradition who said little about God.

No wonder that Friends of God, like Jan van Ruysbroeck and Johann Tauler, spoke out against the aberrations. They had to do so in pure self-defense. For the church could make no distinction between "Mystik" and "Mysticismus," between the mystical theology that is experiential wisdom in Christ, on the one hand, and a God-talk that breeds licentiousness and ethical insensitivity on the other. Throughout the 1300s and the 1400s the established church battled against the Free Spirits. But The Friends of God were often included in the harsh judgment and the severe treatment. Yet the Friends are definitely to be distinguished from the Free Spirits. Ruysbroeck, one of the Friends, wrote about the Free Spirits: "They live in mortal sin, not troubling themselves about God or His grace, but thinking that virtue is sheer nonsense and that the spiritual life is hypocrisy and delusion. They hear with disgust all mention of God or virtue, for they are persuaded that there is no such thing as God, or heaven, or hell. They acknowledge but what is palpable to the senses."

After the Reformation the groups of Free Spirits died out. But the issue is still with us. *Theologia Germanica* sharpens it in this manner: Are we elevating man to be the eternal God or are we saying that man should turn to and grow in the eternal God while living in the world?

Theologia Germanica's History Among Protestants

Formally speaking *Theologia Germanica* still belongs to the reading material a Roman Catholic ought to shun. We had occasion to treat this question at the end of the section on The Friends of God, since it is connected with the official ecclesiastical attitude to medieval revivals of various kinds.

It remains to ask how the people of the Reformation reacted to the little book.[25]

Let us first repeat that the *Theologia* must have been much read and appreciated in the sixteenth and seventeenth centuries. It appeared in twenty editions during Martin Luther's lifetime. Its influence diminished in the age of rationalism and Enlightenment and then increased again in the nineteenth century.

Since our account will focus in particular on Protestant reactions to the book we shall only register in passing that Luther's early father confessor, Johann Staupitz, learned much from Tauler and the *Theologia*. The third well-known "disciple" was Andreas Bodenstein, called Carlstadt after the town from which he hailed. Carlstadt spoke in the manner of *Theologia Germanica* about that sign of a faith-borne will called *Gelassenheit*, "inner serenity." In *Theologia*'s style he used the terms *Meinheit* and *Sichheit*, the sin-filled concentration on the concerns of the me and the self. He acknowledged directly his indebtedness to *Theologia*.

Both Carlstadt and Luther grounded their evaluation

of the devotional book in the depth of evangelical faith—although Carlstadt of course soon enough parted company with Luther on essential issues. But *Theologia Germanica* became a symbol for antiecclesial forces of the Reformation, the Enthusiasts or the Schwärmer. The Enthusiasts did not refer to *Theologia* on account of its religious-ethical message in the first place. What struck them was probably rather that the book speaks directly of sacraments only in Chapter 23. It seemed to consider preaching on the basic religious attitude as a means of grace in itself. Since the Enthusiasts had become persuaded that no external "signs" are necessary in the life of a Christian they rated a relative silence about the sacraments as a proof of the correctness of their own views. Luther had, after all, highly recommended the book. The tractates of the Schwärmer and Anabaptists are filled with allusions to *Theologia*. Parenthetically it should be noted that the Schwärmers' argument from silence is, like all such arguments, rather tenuous, especially since we know that The Friends of God deliberately pointed to the orders of the church as helpful means in the life of earnest Christ-followers. We should also draw attention to the importance *Theologia* placed on the use of external "images."

Denck, Hetzer, Schwenckfeldt—all of them leaders in either Anabaptist or mystical-pietistic circles—thought highly of *Theologia*. Denck and Hetzer initiated a new print of it in 1555. Sebastian Franck occupied himself intensively with *Theologia Germanica*. He translated it into Latin attaching his own paraphrases and comments. These additions have a spiritualistic ring. Franck counterposes the external and the internal in religion and by and large rejects the external. In a preface he invests *Theologia* with the highest authority, next to the Bible. Valentin Weigel is perhaps the one among the sixteenth-century Lutherans of a mystical bent who used *Theologia* most. His devotional writing is very close to the Frankfurter's language. He is rumored to have written an introduction to the ideas of *Theologia* but, if so, we do not have copies of it today.

On Reformed ground Sebastian Castellio was drawn to the Frankfurther's message. Independently of Franck he translated the book into Latin. He found it to be a healthy antidote to Calvinistic rigor. His preface revolves around the following theme: To love God on account of His benefactions, that is to say, out of thankfulness, is not the perfect way of Christian living. Man must love God without egotism and "me-dom," not because He does good things for us but because He is good in Himself.

The rationalistic ring of Reformed theology prevented it from hearing anything worthwhile in *Theologia Germanica.* Guillaume Farel wrote that it had to originate with archheretic David Joris, the worst pejorative in Farel's vocabulary. The printer in Basle is taken to task for having published such a "godless" work. German Christianity is in a bad way, Farel continued, when such Anabaptist errors could be regarded as theology of true faith. We are being led away from God to mere contemplation.

Calvin was no less sharp in his judgment about "*Theologia Germanica* and the new man." In a letter to the Reformed congregation in Frankfurt he says that, if he understood anything at all of the word of God—and he hoped, of course, that the congregation would grant him that he did indeed—what is said in *Theologia* is of such a nature that the congregation would do well in never laying hold of the book. "For, although there are no outstanding errors in it, it contains frivolities, conceived by Satan's cunning in order to confuse the whole simplicity of the gospel. And if you look deeper into it you will find that it contains a hidden deadly poison which can poison the church. Therefore, my brethren, shun like the pest all those who try to defile you with such impurities."

INTRODUCTION

Theodore Beza, Calvin's friend and supporter of the death sentence against Miguel Servet, took a very dim view of the publication of *Theologia* on Swiss territory. And what Calvin and Beza had said about the book became the accepted verdict in the church. In the 1700s a well-known Reformed theologian accused Luther of irresponsibility and lack of wisdom for having given the *Theologia* such high marks. He placed the work on the same low level as Bale-theologian Oecolampadius's recommendation of a tractate by Schwenckfeldt.

In the Lutheran camp the appraisal was more positive. *Theologia*'s ideas were not considered acceptable at all junctures but the Lutheran interpretation of the life of faith no doubt embraced some of the Frankfurter's major points. That this favorable judgment was not merely an expression of loyalty to Father Martin himself is evidenced by the fact that Mathias Flacius, staunch defender of "objective" salvation, included *Theologia Germanica* in his list of "testifiers to the truth." Flacius was especially impressed with Chapters 9, 37 and 49, where salvation is ascribed to God alone. He makes it a point to remind his readers that Luther had praised the book since it teaches correctly about sin, free will, the old man, and also about grace, Christ, and rebirth.

The organist, jurist, poet, and theologian Nicolaus Selnecker, who started out close to Melanchthon's ideas but later became more orthodox, referred to the "excellent thoughts of *Theologia Germanica*, edited by J. Arndt . . . our special friend." Selnecker, who was centrally involved in the work on the Formula of Concord, wrote that the book propounds the thought that God does not love Himself as Himself but rather as the highest Good and in the same way we should love God and only so become good.

But the climate changed and as we enter the seventeenth century Lutheran orthodoxy grows increasingly wary of *Theologia Germanica*. Nikolaus Hunnius's opinion was guarded. He vigorously defended orthodox, objective concepts of Justification, original sin, and the sacraments against the assaults of Lutheran Enthusiasts like Valentin Weigel. In the process he had to take a stand on *Theologia* and on Johann Tauler, who meant a great deal to Weigel and Weigelians. This was his conclusion: The Frankfurter's tractate served a useful purpose in its own time as a refutation of heresies concerning the free will. It discounted good works as a help toward salvation; it removed man's claim that his own natural endowment and free will are parts of redemption. After all, was not this just what Luther wanted to say? In *Theologia Germanica*, Hunnius pointed out, one could not find any of Weigel's delusions. Yet should the church apply Luther's yardstick to *Theologia*, the book would have to be rejected. For did not Luther measure the worth of the Epistle of James with the truth of Christ's merit? Hunnius could not tolerate *Theologia* expressions like the one about God's becoming "humanized" in the faithful or the one about the possibility of satan, if truly converted, turning into an angel.[26] The Lutheran schoolman was also perturbed over *Theologia*'s suggestion that no one can enter the Christ life and the Christ light by reading and study, the dictum that God loves Himself only because He is the perfect Good, the assertion that the faithful and Godlike are in need of no commands. Nor did he understand *Theologia*'s talk about *Gelassenheit*, "carefree serenity." On the whole, Nikolaus Hunnius declared, in "our time and age," the seventeenth century, one could safely dispose of such books.

But Luther's power of judgment in theological matters could not be wholly neglected. With a bow in the Reformer's direction, seventeenth-century schoolman Johann Benedict Carpzow suggested that Father Martin's

28

opinion should be understood not in an absolute but in a relative sense. It was essential to see it in relation to scholastic Roman theology. Looked at in this fashion *Theologia* must be said to offer quests for a piety for which there was no room in arid scholasticism. The work was not, Carpzow felt, "purely mystical" but rather "a wonderfully purified little brook." It could still help Christians by offering the best of what mystical theologians have said.

Johann Franz Buddeus, at the end of the seventeenth and the beginning of the eighteenth century, declared from his chair as professor in Jena that many are unable to underwrite all dicta in *Theologia Germanica* and for this he had understanding. Yet the book is "excellent and filled with good fruit."

The hesitancy on the part of Lutheran orthodoxy should, of course, also be seen against the background that *Theologia* had been read so avidly and referred to so consistently by Schwärmer, who found the book's emphasis on the inner life a support for their assaults against outer forms of religion. They had almost wrecked the beginnings of the Reformation. The connection between radicals and *Theologia* must have influenced the verdicts of orthodox Lutherans.

But there is that other current of Lutheran religious life, commonly described as "pietism." The Lutheran pietists emphasized that they were well within Doctor Martin's legacy when they stressed the place of personal piety and subjective spirituality in the Christian economy of salvation. The Lutherans of the inner life were by and large responsible for the continued sequence of *Theologia* editions in the century during which mystical theological writings were not much in vogue (the eighteenth). *Theologia Germanica* became a well-accepted book among pietists. One of their leaders, Gottfried Arnold, wrote in his *Impartial History of Church and Heresy* that, whether or not one is satisfied with Luther's stance, it should be clear what the Reformer wanted to say by publishing *Theologia*. He wanted to say that he had tasted the power of the book and found it consonant with his experience. It would therefore, Arnold maintained, be futile to keep on papering over or qualifying the theological verdict and the subsequent action of our father in the faith.

Johann Arndt, author of the famous *True Christianity*, stressed in his teaching and preaching the "Christ in us" not to the exclusion of but in a justified reaction against the "Christ for us" theology of orthodox Lutherans. He represented "a genuine Lutheran mysticism" (Kirke-Leksikon), orthodox with respect to pure doctrine, yet a proponent of inner "heart theology." It is therefore no surprise that Arndt was responsible for an edition of the *Theologia*. In the preface to it he points out that *Theologia* emphasizes life, not conceptual formulations. He finds this excellently done.

Christian Scriver refers to the Frankfurter's work in his *Seelenschatz* and his words are full of praise.

Philipp Jakob Spener, "the father of German pietism," speaks warmly in favor of *Theologia Germanica* both in his *Pia Desideria* and in his foreword to Tauler's works.

Thus within the Lutheran church we observe, on the one hand, an increasingly skeptical attitude to the message of *Theologia Germanica* with orthodoxy and, on the other, warm approval among the pietists.

The same holds true of the Calvinistic movement. Whereas the founders and later dogmaticians were opposed to it, for doctrinal reasons, Reformed pietists read *Theologia* with inner recognition. Pierre Poiret, eighteenth-century mystic and minister in southern Germany, published editions in French. Dogmatic opposition against Arndt and Spener often included attacks on *Theologia*. Reformed theologians found it difficult to explain

INTRODUCTION

Luther's esteem for the book and took the same way out as their orthodox colleagues in the Lutheran camp: They opined that Luther's opinion was "relative" and must be seen as a word *against* scholasticism.

As we have said, the age of rationalism saw a decline in mystical theology although editions of *Theologia* continued to appear during the 1700s, in German, Swedish, Dutch, and Latin.

Among those who edited *Theologia Germanica* in the first half of the 1800s was Troxler, who in his introduction draws attention to the Frankfurter's ethical dualism between the natural and the supernatural man. In the editor's opinion this was a dualism vastly different from the dichotomy between spirit and nature in Catholic thinking. Troxler himself seems to have been leaning toward the Enthusiasts in his theological reflection. A few years later Biesenthal prefaced his edition by declaring: "The content can of course not appeal to all factions with equal strength, especially not to run-of-the-mill rationalism." This would apply especially to the idea about the God-man, which "to rationalism, can be at the most a symbol of spiritual and moral conditions. The book ought to be particularly welcome to the inward piety and profound speculation of our days" (1842). Persons of such inclinations "will feel at home with the *Theologia*." For *Theologia*'s piety vibrates on their principles, its teaching being centered in "self-denial, humility, and divine blessedness."

Wilhelm de Wette, famous exegete and systematic theologian, said in his *Christian Ethics* (last volume 1823) that *Theologia* is an admirable, sound, pithy tract, full of spirit and life, written in a direct, solid language and indeed worthy of the recommendation Luther gave it. Hegelian philosopher Johann Rosenkranz points to the fact, not to be neglected by the learned, that the constant reprinting of the book, from Luther, Spener, and onward, is a proof of its "worth" and "indispensability." J. E. Erdmann in the field of philosophy of history, F. G. Lisco in the field of biblical theology, and Christian Bunsen, diplomat, linguist, and dogmatician—all of them spoke with warmth about the spiritual weight of *Theologia Germanica.*

Bunsen commands special interest in our context, as he was the one who caused *Theologia* to be translated and printed in England. Susanna Winkworth made the translation and Bunsen wrote a "Letter to the Translator," which can be found in the English edition, to which references are made at several points in the present book. "I rank this short treatise," writes Bunsen, "with Luther, next to the Bible, but unlike him, should place it before rather than after St. Augustine. That school of pious, learned, and profound men of which this book is, as it were, the popular catechism . . . was the first protest of the Germanic mind against the Judaism and formalism of the Byzantine and medieval churches, the hollowness to which scholasticism had led, and the rottenness of society which a pompous hierarchy strove in vain to conceal, but had not the power nor the will to correct. Eckart and Tauler, his pupil, brought religion home from fruitless speculation, and reasonings upon imaginary or impossible suppositions, to man's own heart and to the understanding of the common people. . . . Let me . . . state . . . the principle of the golden book which you are just presenting to the English public, in what I consider, with Luther, the best theological exponent, in plain Teutonic, thus: Sin is selfishness: Godliness is unselfishness: a godly life is the stedfast working out of inward freeness from self: To become thus godlike is the bringing back of man's first nature . . . We must scorn all idea of reward . . . this small but golden Treatise has been now for almost forty years, an unspeakable comfort to me and to many Christian friends ... to whom I had the happiness of introducing it. ..."

Charles Kingsley also contributes a preface to Winkworth's translation. He says he honors the book especially because of "its noble views of righteousness and of sin." The book, he continues, will be of little use to those who are Christians in order to come to eternal bliss in an afterlife. It is for those who desire "to be freed ... while they live on earth."

There were and are of course forms of Protestant theology, in both the nineteenth and twentieth century, that find little to fetch in *Theologia*. The reason is primarily that these systems have no room for "mystical theology." The tradition evolving from Schleiermacher, influenced as it was by the intellectualistic mood it addressed in apologetic ways, belongs to this category. A great deal of historical-critical reflection on revelation has been equally insensitive to the mystical aspects of Luther's and the Friends' thought. So-called neo-orthodox thinking spearheaded by Karl Barth has shown scant interest in the traditions of piety and mystical experience, "outlawing" them from what is considered "objective" system building, on the strength of two major a priori suppositions: first, that "transcendence," from a theological point-of-view, can never imply a "going-out-of-time", second, that even religiously motivated moral life and ethical thought must be rooted in the kind of self-autonomy that in fact renders irrelevant the simple God-attachment and inner detachment that are the concerns of piety and mystical theology.

One sign of the impact this Western theological intellectualism has had on the selection of material deemed worthy of printing in English is the fact that only Winkworth of the year 1854, Bernhart, in English since 1949, and the Th. Kepler translation of 1952 have been available. The latest reprint of Winkworth is dated 1937, the latest of Bernhart 1951, and the latest of Kepler 1961(?).[27] As far as I have been able to ascertain, all three of them are out of print at the time of writing (1979). It should also be noted that all three of them are based on the Würzburg manuscript of 1497, not on Luther's manuscript.

Perhaps our devotional tract has been so relatively unobtainable during the past quarter century in part because mystical theology and devotional concentration are judged to have little or nothing to do with the grounding of Christian ethics. A few words will therefore be devoted to the question whether this is so in *Theologia Germanica.*

The Grounding of Ethics in Theologia Germanica

Any theology that endeavors to include in its purview the element called *sapientia experimentalis,* the experience of the presence of God, a presence not only in history in general but in heart and mind, encounters the objection that, since it is fundamentally engaged in a flight from the world, it cannot possibly take a serious interest in the world.

This is not the place to mount a large-scale refutation of the accuracy of this generalization. Like all generalizations it harbors both truth and error. About *Theologia Germanica,* a book of what happens to the soul before the throne of God, we can say that it does not enjoin us to escape the world for the sake of escaping it but rather to take some rest from it in God in order better to deal with it in deed.

Recognize the Good Earth
Theologia Germanica brings a positive message about the earth and incarnated existence. Its dualism is a dual-

ism between self-will and God's will, not between nature and spirit. God's living presence here on earth is more important to the Frankfurter than the idea that God's spirit stands over against the material world. "God is all-embracing Goodness," he says. "Hence ... all things are good. ... Nothing but sin is contrary to God" (Chapter 34). "In the very depth of it all nothing is contrary to God or contrary to the true Good" (Chapter 42). "Everything in our existence is truly a precinct of the Eternal or Eternity." We have a great many "signs of God and Eternity" here among us and they provide "directions and paths to God and Eternity." Everything in creation "is a welcome to you and permitted, as long as it does not take place for your own gain or in accordance with your own will but flows out of and is in accordance with my [God's] will" (Chapter 47).

In other words, *Theologia* ascribes a profound significance to the material existence and this significance is positive, not negative In fact, life on earth is an essential part of "God Himself." The orders and rules of this earth constitute His relationship with us (Chapter 37).

What difference does this life-in-God on earth make for the ethos of living?

The Ethics of the Changed Soul

Instead of the transcendental notion of God in scholasticism we meet in *Theologia* the message of the living, present God. The human self is asked to make room for this living, present God.

The soul can make room for the living God only by surrendering its self-will. If "all beings are in truth one in the perfect Being," it follows that "the farther we are from this realization, the farther we are from the right path." The great obstacle to genuine moral living is this: "Man will seek his own good, what he considers his own best, as though it were his possession and had to be for his own personal sake and emanated from himself" (Chapter 42). Our self-will becomes attached to a particular thing in this world, is swallowed up by it, loses sight of God's love, which is "love for all things in One" (Chapter 44). Yes, "all humans are bent upon the self . . ." (Chapter 24). The Frankfurter's ethics was as realistic as Luther's. The Reformer spoke of man as a creature "curved in on himself."

But when we become aware of our sinfulness before the throne of God and surrender to Him, a reduction of our self ensues. Out of this comes humility before God and man and that humility is the beginning of God-guided morality (Chapter 33).

A change of disposition has occurred. You do not become a friend of God and a disciple of Christ by adding a new moral code to your life. You become a friend when your soul changes from proud to humble. Nor is it a matter of acquiring knowledge about "the difference between virtue and wickedness." It is rather a matter of loving virtue because of the experience of God's love. You are in a new frame of mind. The one who is not in that frame of mind "is not truly moral" despite external probity and many correct ideas (Chapter 39).

This move toward true ethical responsibility means that the soul trustingly surrenders a goodly portion of its self-will. But this does not mean that the self is extinguished. The self was created by God. It is meant to serve God and man during its earthly sojourn. The self is still there, minus part of its self-will. In some generalizations of mystical theology we read that mysticism always aims at "extinction of the I or the self." That is not so. The Frankfurter speaks about the change of the soul that initiates true moral life. You are struck down but you rise again, a different person, also ethically.

A difference prevails between the ethics of ordinary, uncrucified existence and the ethics of those who have been led into the path of surrender and cross taking. We can call the latter the ethics of the second mile.

The Ethics of the Second Mile

Theologia Germanica, like many mystical writings in medieval and in modern times, seems to lay little direct stress on Christ's redemption, the "for you" of salvation. It is more interested in the other side of salvation, the Christ "in you." We have already touched on this matter in passing. Here we have an opportunity to return to the question for a moment. The Frankfurter does have an intuition about that part of God's self-disclosure which brings us the "for you," the vicarious nature of Christ's suffering and the vicarious nature of true Christian responsibility-taking. Christ is described from this point of view (Chapter 13). When speaking about "righteousness" the Frankfurter maintains that if one "is the enemy of unrighteousness, he becomes prepared to suffer and act vicariously wherever he detects unrighteousness in a fellow-being, striving to remove the unjust condition . . ." (Chapter 39). In other words, ethical responsibility can entail vicarious deeds, actions that involve some kind of suffering. For the moral life often includes the unpopular cause: to react against unrighteousness. The declaration that loving God means loving "all things in one" is not meant to be only a safe philosophical observation. The Frankfurter thinks it must be translated into deeds. Those deeds are, like the deeds of our Lord, of a vicarious nature: walking that second mile, turning the other cheek.

Luther spoke in the same vein about the grounding of Christian ethics. It was more than rational decision making. It was living for and with others under the cross. Christian deeds in the world, said Luther, are the extension of the work that "Christ merely initiated." The Christians, he continued, are people who trustingly lean on Christ and by His power become vicarious helpers to the whole world. This is not apparent to the beneficiaries. Christians look like "poor beggars," yet they possess everything. The world is unaware of the power of vicarious spiritual involvement and "thank the Christians poorly for it." Ungodly people receive benefits from "the spiritual rule" of Christians in Christ's name and power. Luther comes close to the Frankfurter's way of speaking about the Christian mystery of invisible engagement in and for the welfare of mankind, both physical and spiritual. Just like the Frankfurter, Luther asserts that this mission can only be carried out by people who have gone through hell with Christ and learned some lessons about humility.[28]

The Place of Rule in the Moral Life

The truly ethical, *Theologia Germanica* maintains, is both rule-free and rule-bound. Against the Free Spirits the Frankfurter defends rule and order. "Since this overgrown spiritual pride," he says about their claim that a truly religious person is bound by no restrictions whatever, "includes the belief that Scripture or doctrine is not essential, the proud ones consider as nought all the rules, orders, laws, and sacraments of the Holy Church; yes, it makes a mockery of them and of all who observe and revere these supports" (Chapter 23). The Free Spirits also argue that moral rules are not binding for those who have seen the light as they claim to have (Chapter 37).

But rule and order are essential ingredients in a moral life. "Human laws and commands belong to the outer man. They are needed when one knows nothing better. Else people would not know what to do and what to omit and become like dogs or cattle" (Chapter 37).

However, when man becomes reduced as to self-will and surrenders to God he is in a sense beyond law and rule. "The illumined ones" know that moral deeds do not a good man make. Only surrendering to God does. They do not perform good deeds expecting reward.

Yet on the other side of the experience by the burning bush the person who has come to know the Lord a little better realizes that order and law belong to his life as a moral person, only in a new manner. "God loves deeds," he can then say, "but not all deeds." He loves those deeds "that grow out of the teachings and instructions of the true Light and the true Love." Deeds done from within that deep rest in God "please Him greatly" (Chapter 45). As you can speak of newborn lives so you can speak of newborn rules.

Martin Luther summed up the problem of order in man's life by saying that a Christian is the freest person of all and bound to none but also the most bound of all and subject to all. A goodly portion of this hard-to-grasp truth is present in *Theologia*.

Contemporary discussions about the grounding of Christian ethics deal with the distinction between "act-agapism" and "rule-agapism." That distinction is in many ways close to the problem that faced mystics and moralists five hundred years ago. Is morality a matter merely of the individual act, in separation from past and future? Or is the divine agape also partly lodged in the rules that are conveyed to us by tradition and community? The Frankfurter would certainly agree with the latter suggestion. However, he would add that all rules are transcended under the tutelage of Christ. For rules as external law have then disappeared. "In this sense we should also understand Saint Paul when he says: Those who are instructed, prompted, and led by the Spirit of God are God's children and are in a way not under the law" (Chapter 28).

Carry and Be Carried: The Secret of Ethical Responsibility

Theologia Germanica suggests that we shall not be able to carry burdens unless we ask to be carried. It is not easy for proud man to accept such a close relationship between the moral life and life in God. When familiarity with problems and people threatens to breed contempt; when the subjection to others, under which we actually live, becomes almost unbearable; when unrighteousness seems to yield not a bit in the face of our pleadings and protests— then we shall realize that the moral challenge of faith involves much more than rational decision making. It involves help from a present, invisible Lord. The experience of this presence will renew love and hope; we shall become young again. It is not in the absence of realistic life experience that the Frankfurter utters the following words, it is in spite of them: "In the heart of a divinized person love is undefiled and unadulterated, borne by good will toward all humans and all created things. Therefore, from within this purity, mankind and all created things must be sincerely loved and one must will and wish and do what is best for them" (Chapter 31).

It must have been from within such an experience that Martin Luther declared that he really never in the depth of his heart hated anyone, quite a statement coming as it did from a man who expended a lot of vitriol in his defense of the evangelical cause. But he knew, from depths beyond the purely rational, that Christ lives, watches, and guards in the *invisibilis*. That could be felt during numerous waves of persecution, in attacks of anguish, and when fear of death by assassination set in. Luther knew, as one can know only by faith beyond belief, that he was carried in order to carry. Christian ethics, which is the residue in thought emerging from moral struggle, must always be aware of the surd behind all logical calculation. Prayer-filled cross bearing is at the heart of Christian moral commitment. What would he do if he knew that the world might come to an end very soon, Luther was once reportedly asked. His answer: plant an apple tree. It is this sort of holy defiance that pervades

Theologia Germanica and fired the imagination of Martin Luther. The odds are heavily against Christ's dream about us. Yet, He knows that the dream will become, more and more powerfully, flesh and blood. "May we," writes the Frankfurter, "abandon our selfish ways and die away from our own will and live only to God and His will. May we be helped to this by Him who surrendered His will . . . and who lives and rules with God, the Father, in union with the Holy Spirit, in perfect Trinity."

Why Luther's Edition Was Chosen

The devotional book now submitted in a new English translation is a product of fourteenth-century piety. When Martin Luther saw it for the first time in 1516, he decided that it was worthy of wider distribution. The work, now commonly known as *Theologia Germanica* [The German theology] became Luther's very first publication.

However, these meditations on life in God and life in the world and their relationship to each other had no specific title and no name of an author when Luther discovered them in handwritten form toward the end of 1516. The manuscript used by Luther probably came from East Prussia.[29] Luther handed over the little book to Gruenenberg, the printer in Wittenberg, with the same general name as it had when it was rediscovered: *Eyn geystlich edles Buchleynn*. The Reformer surmised that "the illumined doctor Tauler" might have had something to do with the origin.[30]

This 1516 edition was shorter than the one that constitutes the basis for the present book. It started with Chapter 7 and ended with Chapter 24 of the present book.

The printing of the 1516 manuscript was completed on December 4, 1516. Ten days later Luther wrote to Spalatin sending him a copy, praising the content of the book as something that helped underscore the central thrust of the gospel.[31]

Luther added a preface to the old document. It is interesting to compare it with the preface found in the present version of 1518. Here follow Luther's words of 1516:

> First of all, this little book warns all those who wish to read and understand its message, especially those of bright intellect and sophisticated reason, that they should not precipitately rush to swift judgment only because it appears awkward in its choice of words or speaks in the way of ordinary preachers and teachers. Indeed, this book does not float on top, like foam on water. It has rather been fetched out of the rock bottom of Jordan by a true Israelite whose name only God knows and whoever is informed about it by God. For it has been found without title and name. But if we should try a guess, the material almost resembles the style of the illumined Doctor Tauler of the Preaching Order. Be that as it may, here we have the true solid teaching of Holy Writ. One has to choose between calling it all a folly and becoming a fool, as the Apostle Paul indicates in 1 Cor. 1: We preach Christ, a folly to the heathen but to those who are called, the wisdom of God.
>
> F. Martinus Luder
> Subscripsit[32]

The suggestion has been made that Luther found the total manuscript already in 1516 but preferred to publish only part of it. This is unlikely. The content of the allegedly omitted sections would certainly gainsay this proposition. Moreover, the later and larger edition (1518) is based on an orthography quite different from that of the smaller book. This fact applies also to the segments that the "Small Theologia" of 1516 has in common with the "Large Theologia" of 1518.[33]

Luther provided his first published work, the briefer version of *Theologia Germanica,* with Latin comments in the margin at three places.[34] The marginal notes are in themselves an indication that Luther actually published what he had in front of him, that is to say, he did not subject his find to editorial pruning.

*   *   *

What has here been called the Large Theologia appeared in 1518 from the same printing shop in Wittenberg that turned out the smaller version. Luther had in the meantime found the total manuscript. He wrote another and longer preface. The book also appeared in separate printed form both in Leipzig and in Augsburg that year. The Wittenberg edition consists of two prints, with slight differences between them. For my translation I have used a copy of print II, Wittenberg, 1518. Its authenticity can be verified with the aid of tools provided by recent bibliographical research.[35]

This time, Luther decided in favor of a real title. He called the book *Eyn Deutsch Theologia,* [a German theology] and let the subtitle describe the content: the right understanding as to what Adam and Christ mean and how Adam must die within us and Christ rise.

The manuscript apparently came from the Carthusian monastery in Erfurt.[36] The table of contents can be assumed to have had the same place in the original Erfurt manuscript as it has in the present version. In other words, Luther handed it over to the readers in the form in which he found it. This also holds true of the book's introduction of the anonymous author. In the manuscript it was evidently combined with the table of contents.[37]

As we saw in connection with the Small Theologia, Luther originally entertained the thought that Johann Tauler might be the author. In the Large Theologia Tauler is quoted and this removes the possibility that he was the author. However, Tauler was no doubt an essential spiritual source for the one who wrote the meditations.

The Luther editions of *Theologia Germanica* (1516 and 1518) were thus based on handwritten documents in monastic libraries. These manuscripts have not been found. The shorter one was a fragment, at one time thought to be the whole. The longer one, rather than being an addition, is simply what must be regarded as the entire work.[38] Before the Gutenberg revolution in printing they were clearly available only to a very limited number of readers, most of them monks, nuns, and priests. Luther wanted to change this. He says in his foreword that many people in the past had not been spiritually amenable to the truths propounded by the book. However, now its time had come.

Luther's feeling that the devotional book he had found would be accepted in a new climate of spiritual yearning proved to be accurate. Already in 1518 two additional editions of the Large Theologia appeared outside Wittenberg, one in Leipzig and one in Augsburg. The Augsburg edition was the first to be equipped with the name that has become the standard title in German: *Theologia Teütsch*, or *Theologia Deutsch*. Before Luther's death in 1546 the Large Theologia was printed in 20 editions.[39] Up to 1961 the book had appeared in 190 editions in twelve languages.[40] However, as we shall see a little later in this Introduction, the English versions, like some of the others, were not based on the manuscript Luther had in front of him but on a printed version of 1497, different in style if not in content.

The name *Theologia Germanica*, a direct latinization of the German title, became increasingly accepted from the latter part of the 1500s. The first edition under this rubric was Swiss and its year of publication 1557.[41]

Before 1851 the various versions of our fourteenth-century devotional tract presented, more or less faithfully, the Luther edition we have now mentioned. But in that year Franz Pfeiffer published a recently discovered version of *Theologia Germanica* that to many appeared less "edited" than the Luther editions. That, too, was a handwritten document, discovered by a professor in Würzburg, hence referred to as the Würzburg edition. Four years later Pfeiffer published a second, improved edition of Würzburg.[42] The Würzburg version of the Large Theologia is dated 1497.

*   *   *

After the discovery of the 1497 manuscript there was a tendency in learned circles to consider the Würzburg version of *Theologia Germanica* more authentic than the manuscripts Luther had at his disposal. A prominent translator, Bernhart, says about Luther's version that "it is logically more sharply arranged than Würzburg, here and there conceptually clarified." Luther, he maintains, probably did not do this "without personal input." It was assumed that Luther acted "as critical redactor, merciless against weak lines and repetitions." It cannot be proved that Luther had found a "more original or older version," this translator continues. "On the contrary, there is evidence . . . that we are here dealing with a sister companion to ours [Würzburg]."[43]

The same translator originated a trend in the way in

which scholars and other translators came to look at the sources behind *Theologia Germanica*. He asserted that his choice of original text cannot "quite match that of Luther's with respect to precision and firmness but precisely because of this it obviously comes closer to the manner in which the various trends of thought were initially committed to paper."[44]

However, new research has thrown a different light on the problem of *Theologia Germanica*'s textual origin. It has thus been asserted that "Luther's texts are by far closest to the origin." It is precisely "the greater succinctness" of the Luther texts that warrants this assumption.[45] Already in the first volume of the Weimar edition of Luther's works the suggestion is made that "Pfeiffer's text [Würzburg] is considerably inferior to the Luther texts."[46] A planned publication of a heretofore unknown manuscript of 1477 will, maintains Baring, prove as false "what has been written about the greater reliability of the 1497 manuscript edited by Pfeiffer, over against Luther's printed editions."[47]

Hermann Mandel wrote in the beginning of the twentieth century that "the time has finally come when Luther's text should be rehabilitated, on account of its scientific value for scientific ends, but also on account of its value for the general public."[48] Yet, the present volume constitutes the first attempt to offer Luther's *Theologia Germanica* text in modern English.

As indicated, in addition to the 1516 and 1518 Luther editions there is a third source, a manuscript of 1497 termed the Würzburg manuscript. Let us have a closer look at it.

The manuscript that has proved most appealing to translators since its discovery at the middle of the nineteenth century is precisely, and perhaps surprisingly, the most elaborate one of the three. Professor Reuss in Würzburg was the first scholar to report the find. The manuscript had been hidden away in the library of the Cistercian monastery at Wertheim on the Tauber and the Main, which later became the electoral library of Bronnbach.

If the dating of the initial handwritten document is somewhat correct, the middle of the 1300s—and judging by the references to Johann Tauler this cannot be too far off—then the Würzburg copy is of "an unfortunately rather recent origin."[49]

This new find—made in the nineteenth century—contains a different orthography and lacks some sentences present in the Large Theologia of 1518, sentences that are then supplanted with others. The most conspicuous trait of Würzburg is, however, the elaborations it contains in comparison with the Luther manuscript of 1518. The two last paragraphs of Chapter 12 in the Luther edition have been expanded into two separate chapters, 13 and 14. The 1497 manuscript from then on runs two chapters ahead of Luther's 1518 edition, until we come to Chapter 48, at which point the Luther edition begins to overtake Würzburg so that in the end we have 56 Luther chapters and 54 Würzburg chapters. The details of additions and overlappings will not be discussed here but at numerous points in the course of our translation references will be made in the footnotes to differences between the Luther and Würzburg texts.

As indicated, Franz Pfeiffer had the Würzburg edition printed in 1851.[50] Pfeiffer gave it too high a rating. He created a somewhat false impression by announcing that he was editing *Theologia Germanica* on the basis of the only manuscript extant. The expression obscures the fact that, indirectly, we have after all two additional sources.[51]

The Pfeiffer Würzburg text does by and large follow the same intentions as the Luther text. But there are some significant differences. I do not think of a certain wordiness in the first place or an obvious eagerness to explicate. But instead of speaking of "sin," as does the Luther text, Würzburg prefers "sins," sometimes dutifully enumerated. Instead of "devil" Würzburg uses "the evil spirit." "Virtue and good outside the soul," as nonproductive of true virtue, receive explicating comment, a kind of second-thought didactic. On the whole, the Luther texts are more terse. As we have said, there is no reason to believe that Luther changed anything essential in the manuscripts he found. We are indeed very close to the source when we read the Luther texts. It is therefore difficult to agree with Joseph Bernhart when he puts the Würzburg manuscript of *Theologia Germanica* before the Luther text on account of the allegedly superior explicatory quality or the lesser logical definiteness of the younger manuscript and on the unfounded assumption that Luther rather drastically changed the wording and the structure of the book he found.[52]

The second edition of *Religion in der Geschichte und Gegenwart* of 1927 expresses the opinion that the manuscript of 1497 is closer to the original text. But in 1929 Gottlob Siedel's research led to a reconsideration, confirmed in the 1930s by Edward Schroder's philological investigation, which led to the conclusion: "Detailed examination proves disastrous for the [1497] manuscript; Luther's edition of 1518 without question ends up as the victor."[53]

Notes On This Translation

The present translation of the so-called Luther text has been made from a copy of the Wittenberg edition 1518, which is in my possession. It has been checked for authenticity with the aid of Mandel's, Benzing's, and Baring's bibliographical and text-critical works. A helpful supplementary text has been Mandel's edition of Luther's 1518 edition.

I have divided the text into more paragraphs than the original would allow. Already in the Mandel edition (1908) the paragraphs had become more numerous than in the Wittenberg document. Benzing terms Mandel's division "arbitrary."[54] It is difficult to see why the original's sometimes long stretches of unparagraphed writing should be slavishly followed. My method of breaking up the text into smaller pieces should, I feel, facilitate the reading. In this regard the present translation could be termed even more arbitrary than the Mandel edition.

Since the Würzburg manuscript of *Theologia Germanica* is the basis for earlier English versions I have added the Würzburg text, in footnotes, at points where the younger text provides significant additions or—but those instances are few—at points where Luther's text offers sentences not to be found in Würzburg. However, it should be underlined that these additions from Würzburg, whether verbatim or in paraphrased form, do not add up to the total 1497 text.

Luther's and the Frankfurter's Bible quotations are sometimes in the nature of paraphrases even though presented as direct quotes. I have indicated the difference by omitting quotation marks in the text around such paraphrases and then given our RSV formulation in the corresponding footnote. The original text lacks quotation marks. The claim for "directness" is simply implied by words like "Tauler says," "Now comes a question."

All through the book the personal pronoun "he" is used when "man" in general or "the Christian" or "the unfaithful" is the subject. I started out writing "he or she" wherever "he" appeared but found it extremely cumbersome and decided to limit myself to "he." I hope that the woman reader will have understanding. We should remember that *Theologia* emerged from circles of Christian community where women wielded much influence and where women often constituted the audience, as in the case of Eckhart and Tauler whose homilies were more often than not delivered to nuns. "He" simply stands for "human" or "person," quite in keeping with the biblical information about the creation of mankind: God created man, into male and female did he create them (Gen. 1:27).

When in a quandary about the most adequate way of lifting a medieval German expression over into English I have sometimes turned to and received good counsel from colleagues at the Lutheran Theological Seminary at Gettysburg. I thank them for their willingness to assist. My wife, Pearl, has helped me to steer away from the inclination to employ too many latinized English words. After all, *Theologia Germanica* is written in a still rather inconsistent but refreshingly vernacular German. It deliberately shuns big philosophical terms, quite a feat considering that the very air of religious existence must have been buzzing with learned Latin terms. The Frankfurter was obviously aware of theological problems. But he wished to communicate with people who were less familiar with technical theological vocabulary. I hope that the following translation will be close enough to this vernacular, yet at the same time acceptable to those who read English in the latter part of the twentieth century. In footnotes I have discussed ambiguities around the meaning of some words and also provided explanatory information about people and conditions. The reader who just wishes to contemplate *Theologia*'s wisdom can, no doubt with impunity, leave the footnotes alone.

The Theologia Germanica
of Martin Luther

THE CLASSICS
OF WESTERN
SPIRITUALITY

Preface

We read that Saint Paul, in spite of his lowly and despised status, wrote mighty and fearless letters[1] and testified that his speech was not embellished with ornate and flowery words[2] yet it proved to be full of treasures of knowledge and wisdom.[3]

This is the manner of God's wonders. Look at these wonders and you will find that pompous and vainglorious preachers are never chosen to proclaim God's words. Rather, as it is written, *ex ore infantium*, that is to say, out of the mouths of babes You have most fittingly brought forth Your praise.[4] Again, God's wisdom loosens the tongues of the slow of speech so that they speak most eloquently.[5]

On the other hand, He punishes conceited folk who are offended and irritated by the simple.[6]

Consilium inopis, and so forth. You have shown disrespect for good counsel and teaching because it was conveyed by poor and lowly persons, and so forth.[7]

I point to the above because I want to alert each and every reader of this little book to the danger of harming himself by becoming irritated with its imperfect German and its unembroidered and ungarlanded words.

For this noble little book, poor and unadorned as it is

as far as wording and purely human wisdom are concerned, is all the richer and abundantly precious in true knowledge and divine wisdom. And, if I may speak with biblical foolishness: Next to the Bible and Saint Augustine no other book has come to my attention from which I have learned—and desired to learn—more concerning God, Christ, man, and what all things are.

It is now brought home to me how false it is when many learned people speak disparagingly about us Wittenberg theologians, alleging that we are disseminating novelties. They speak as though there would not have been people in the past and in other places who said what we say.

Indeed, there have been such people. But God's wrath, evoked by our sin, has prevented us from recognizing or hearing them. We were not considered worthy.

For instance, it is clear that their message has not for a long time been treated at our universities. It has gone so far that God's holy word has not only been shoved under the workbench but in fact almost moldered away there, gathering dust and assailed by moths.

Read this booklet, anyone, and determine for yourself whether the theology as we do it in Wittenberg is newfangled or in a solid tradition. This book is certainly not new.

Now, some will perhaps say, as they have done before, that we are German theologians.[8] This is quite all right with us. I thank God that I can hear and find my God in the German tongue, the way I do here, in a manner in which I and the German theologians with me so far did not find Him even in Latin, Greek, or Hebrew.

God grant that this little book may become increasingly known. It will then be confirmed that the German theologians are no doubt the best theologians.[9]

Doctor Martinus Luther
Augustinian at Wittenberg

Now Follows the Table of Contents of the Book

God the Almighty has spoken this little book through a wise, thoughtful, genuinely righteous person, a friend of His. This person was once a German knight, a priest and a warden in the German house of knights in Frankfurt [am Main]. He teaches many wonderful tenets of divine truth and especially how, where, and whereby one might discern those who are in truth God's righteous friends and the unrighteous, false, disorderly spirits who harm the holy church.[10]

will ever do with them in the future. And how blessedness and joy can be found only in God and that which refers to Him in his works, and not in the created beings themselves.

10. How persons who have become whole[12] desire nothing but to be related to the eternal good, in the manner in which the hand is related to the human body. And how such persons have lost their fear of hell and their urge for heaven.

11. How the righteous man in his temporal existence is brought into hell and cannot be comforted there. And how he is taken out of hell and brought into heaven where he cannot be saddened.

12. What proper, true inner peace is, which Christ left with His disciples as His parting gift. How man often lets go of external signs too soon. On three phases that lead man to wholeness.

13. How all men are dead in Adam and have come to life again in Christ. Also, about true obedience and about disobedience.

14. What the old man is and also what the new man is.

15. How we are not to take credit for good things we have done but acknowledge guilt for the evil we have done.

16. How Christ's life was the noblest and best life ever lived and ever to be lived; and how a careless, false, free life is the worst possible life.

17. How one cannot come to the true light and to the Christ life by much questioning or reading or by high natural knowledge and reason but only by renouncing oneself and all things.

18. Since the life of Christ is most bitter to our nature and our self, our nature will not accept it and selects for itself a careless, false way of living, that which is most comfortable and filled with enjoyment.

how He is a light and an understanding and all virtues and how one should hold most dear the highest and best Good.

31. How in a divinized[13] person love is pure and unadulterated and how this love wants to cherish all creatures and do the best possible for them.

32. If man is to attain the best he must let go his self-will and he who goads people to self-will goads to the worst.[14]

33. How in a divinized person there is true humility rooted in the ground of his being and also how there is poverty of spirit.[15]

34. How nothing is contrary to God but sin and what sin is.

35. How there is in God no grief, suffering, dislike, and such but how it is present in a divinized person.

36. How one should put on the Christ life out of love and not for reward and how one should never put it aside or cast it off.

37. How God desires order, rules, moderation, and the like, in His creatures, since He cannot have these without the creatures; also, four kinds of people in their practice of and dealings with order, rules, and good habits.

38. A clear difference demarcating the false light and its characteristics.

39. In what sense that person is called divinized who is transfused by the divine Light and who burns with eternal, divine love; and how light and knowledge are of no avail without love.

40. A question whether one might confess God without loving Him and how there are two kinds of light and love, a true and a false kind.

41. Signs by which one may recognize a truly divinized person and what characterizes such a person; also what characterizes a false light or a false Free Spirit.

42. How nothing else wars against God but self-will and how he who seeks his best as his own good does not find it and how man cannot know or do anything good from himself.
43. Where the Christ life is present Christ is also present. How the Christ life is the very best and noblest life that ever was or can ever be.
44. How complete satisfaction and rest are to be found only in God and in no creatures and how he who wants to be obedient to God must be obedient to all in vicarious long-suffering ways and how he who wants to love God must also love all things in one.
45. Whether one should also love sin when enjoined to love all things.
46. How one must believe several things pertaining to divine truth as a prerequisite before coming to true knowledge and experience.
47. About the self-will and how Lucifer and Adam fell away from God through self-will. How this temporal existence is a paradise and a suburb to the kingdom of heaven and how only one tree is forbidden there, namely self-will.
48. Why God created the self-will seeing that it is so contrary to Him.
49. How we might understand the two words spoken by Jesus, one being this, that "no one comes to the Father except through me," the other that "no one comes to me except that the Father draws him." This he teaches through seven Chapters to the end of the book (50–56).

Chapter 1

Saint Paul says that, when that which is perfect comes, then that which is imperfect and partial is done away with. Note now what the perfect and the partial are. The Perfect is a Being who has comprised and embraced in Himself and in His Being all that is. Without this Being and outside of it there is no true being and in it all things have their being since it is the core of all things.[16]

This ultimate Being is in Himself unchangeable and immovable, yet changes and moves everything else.[17]

But the incomplete and partial originates from or emerges out of total perfection—just as the sun or a light emits radiance and beams—and becomes manifest in one form or another.

None of these parts is perfect. Thus the Perfect is not identifiable with any of its parts.

Creatures that are partial and imperfect can be comprehended, known, and described in words. But the Creator, the Perfect, cannot be comprehended, known, and described in the same manner by creatures, on account of their creatureliness.

The Perfect must consequently be nameless because it is not any created thing.[18]

The creature as created is incapable of discerning, comprehending, naming, or formulating in thought that which is perfect.

Now, when that which is perfect comes, the imperfect will be rejected.

When does it come, then? I say, when it is known and felt and tasted in the soul to the extent possible.[19]

Now one might ask: Since no creatures can know or apprehend the Perfect and since the soul is creaturely, how then can the Perfect be known in the soul?

Answer: That is why we speak of the soul as creature;

that is to say, it is impossible for the creature to know on the basis of its creatureliness, createdness, and I-related-ness. For in whichever creature this perfect life is to be known, creatureliness, createdness, selfishness, must be abandoned and destroyed.

This is what Saint Paul's words mean when he writes that when the Perfect comes—that is when it is known in the heart—then that which only exists in part—creatureliness, createdness, selfishness, impulse-ridden desire—will be spurned and considered nought.[20]

As long as one holds to these things and is cemented to them, the Perfect remains unknown.

Someone might also say: You maintain that there is nothing outside this wholeness, this complete being, or extraneous to it. Yet you also say that something flows out of the Perfect Being; what thus flows out of Him is outside of Him, is it not?

I answer: That is why we say that there is no *true* being outside or without Him. What has flowed out is not true being and has no being except inside the Perfect. It is accidental[21] or a radiance and a beam, which is "being" only in the sense in which a fire, the sun, or a candle light emits radiance.

Chapter 2

The Scriptures, the Truth, and the Faith proclaim that sin is nothing but a turning away on the part of the creature from the unchangeable Good toward the changeable.

This is to say that the creature turns from the Perfect to the imperfect, to separateness, to the partial, and pre-eminently to itself.[22]

Note that when the creature assumes for itself some

good thing, like being, life, knowledge, power—briefly, everything one might term good—as though the creature *were* indeed one of these goods, or as though the Good *belongs* to the creature—in such situations the creature is turning away from God.

Was that not what the devil did? What else did his apostasy and fall consist of but that he assumed for himself that he, too, was something, and that something was his and that something was his own property.[23]

This assumption and his "I" and his "Me" and his "Mine"—that was his apostasy and his fall. And this is still the case.

Chapter 3

What else did Adam do but precisely this thing?

We are used to saying that Adam was lost and fell because he ate that apple.

I say it was because of his presumption and because of his I and his Mine, his Me and the like.

He could have eaten seven apples, yet had this not been connected with his presumption, he would not have fallen.

But he fell at the moment his presumption occurred and that could have happened even if he had not bitten into a single apple.

But listen—I have fallen a hundred times deeper than Adam and strayed a hundred times further. No humans in the world could make amends for or undo Adam's fall and apostasy.

How, then, shall the fall be redeemed? It must be amended like Adam's fall and by the same one who amended Adam's fall, and in the same manner.

By whom or in what manner did this healing take place?

Man could not do it without God and God has not designed to do it without man. Hence God assumed human nature or humanity. He became humanized and man became divinized. That is the way the amends were made.[24]

My fall must be amended in the same way. I cannot do it without God and God does not command or will it without me. For if it is to happen, God must become humanized in me. This means that God takes unto Himself everything that is in me, from within and from without, so that there is nothing in me that resists God or obstructs His work.

Even if God would take to himself all humans in the world and become humanized in them and they would become divinized in Him and this did not happen in me, my fall and my apostasy would never be amended. No, it must also occur in me.[25]

In this return and healing I can, may, or shall do nothing from myself but simply let it happen. This means that God alone works and I suffer His work and His will to take place.[26]

When I do not suffer this to occur but let my I and my Me rule, I hinder God from working alone without obstruction.

Hence my fall and my apostasy remain unredeemed. Lo, my presumption brings all this about.

Chapter 4

God says, "My glory I give to no other."[27] By this He simply means that honor and glory belong to God alone.

When I claim something good as my own achievement, in the belief that I am good, or that I can do the good of myself, or that I know the good, or that I am the one that carries out the good as though it came from me, belongs to me, or is my due, and things along this line, when this happens I usurp merit and honor and commit two evils.

First, there is a falling away and an apostasy, as already pointed out.

Second, I take away some of God's honor and ascribe to myself something that belongs to God alone.

For nothing of that which is worthy of the term *good* belongs to man. It belongs only to the Eternal, to true Goodness. He who claims it himself acts unrighteously and against God.

Chapter 5

Not a few argue that man before God should become free from rules, will, love, knowledge, and so on.[28]

However, this cannot mean that there is no knowledge in man or that God does not become known in man or loved in man, or willed, desired, and praised in man. That would be a great deficiency in God's economy. Then man would be just like cattle, yes indeed like a dumb beast.

No, this way of talking—the voiding of rule, will, and so forth—actually means that acknowledging God becomes so clear and perfect that this knowledge is not man's knowledge or any creature's knowledge but the knowledge of the Eternal, which is to say the eternal Word.[29]

And thus man—or the creature—sets out on a new quest, claiming nothing for his own self. The less he assumes on his own behalf the more perfect and whole he becomes.

Will, love, and desire reflect this change. For the less one claims these powers to oneself the more transparent and divine they become and the more one ascribes them to oneself the baser and more contaminated and imperfect they become.

It is therefore best to rid oneself of those grosser contaminations, that is to say the false claims. To the extent that we do so we begin to have the noblest, clearest knowledge that can ever dwell in man, and also the noblest and purest love and desire. For these powers are then all of God. It is better and nobler that they are of God than of the creature.

That I ascribe some good to myself stems from the illusion that the Good is mine or that I am It. If I had inner knowledge I would indeed know that I am not the Good, that It is not mine, that It does not emanate from me, and so forth. The false assumption would fall off by such knowledge.

It is better that God and things divine be known, loved, and praised even if the worshiper should vainly think that *he* produces the love and the praise—as though God would otherwise remain unpraised, unloved,[30] unhonored, and unknown.

For when the illusion and the ignorance turn into a realization of the Truth, the assumption that the Good comes from us will disappear of its own.

Man will then say, "Look, I poor fool imagined that it was I but, in truth, it is and was God!"

Chapter 6

A master, Boethius by name,[31] says that the fact that we do not love the best stems from a defective condition. He is right. The best ought to be most cherished by us and this love should give no heed to usefulness or uselessness, enhancement or detraction, gain or loss, honor or dishonor, praise or blame, nor anything of the same kind of opposites. But what is truly the noblest and best should also be the dearest and for no other reason than the fact that it is best and noblest.

Man should order his life accordingly both with respect to the external and the internal.[32]

In the external such order should be established because there is a hierarchy among the creatures: One is better than the other with respect to the eternal Good for in one It shines and works more than in the other.

The person in whom the eternal Good most clearly shines, glows, works, is known and loved, is also the best.

And a person in whom the least of this is found is the least good.

Therefore, when in your dealings and relationships with other persons you apply knowledge of such differences, the best creature turns out to be most dear to you. You should hold to those persons and choose their company, especially the ones whose ways one attributes to God, namely that they belong to God, are God's, in goodness, truth, love of peace, righteousness, and the like.

In this manner we can order our outward man and reject and flee from that which wars against the ways of God.

But if our inner being would make a leap into the Perfect, one would find and taste that the Perfect is limitlessly, endlessly, insuperably nobler and better than all imperfect and imcomplete things.[33]

That inner being of ours would also find the Eternal above the transitory and the wellspring and origin underneath everything that flows from it and ever will flow from it.

By this experience we would lose our taste for the imperfect and partial; it would become as nothing. Know this: What I have now described must take place if the noblest and best shall also become that which you love most of all.

Chapter 7

Remember how it is written that the soul of Christ has two eyes, a right eye and a left eye.[34] In the beginning, when these were created,[35] Christ's soul turned its right eye toward eternity and the Godhead and therefore immovably beheld and participated in divine Being and divine Wholeness. This vision continued unmoved and unhampered by all vicissitudes, travail, agitation, suffering, torment, agony—tribulations surpassing anything ever experienced in a person's outer life.

But at the same time the left eye of Christ's soul, his other spiritual vision, penetrated the world of created beings and there discerned distinctions among us, saw which ones were better and which ones were less good, nobler or less noble. Christ's outward being was structured in accordance with such inner discrimination.

Thus Christ's inner being, its vision through the soul's right eye, always participated in full measure in the divine nature, in complete bliss and joy.

But the outer man, the left eye of His soul, was involved in a full measure of suffering, distress, and travail. Yet this took place in such a way that the inner, right eye remained unmoved, unimpeded, untouched by all the travail, suffering, and torment that the outer man had to deal with.

It has been said that Christ, when bound to the pillar and beaten and when hanging on the cross, experienced all this in His outer man, while the inner man, the soul in its function as the right eye, rested in the same bliss and joy as it did after the Ascension or as it does at this very moment.[36]

By the same token Christ's outer man, the soul in its function as the left eye, was never impeded or weakened in its discharge of external duties. The one does not wait for the other.

Now, the created soul of man also has two eyes. One represents the power to peer into the eternal. The other gazes into time and the created world, enabling us to distinguish between the lofty and the less lofty, as I said above.

But these two eyes, which are parts of man's soul, cannot carry out their functions simultaneously. If the soul is looking into eternity through its right eye, the left eye must cease all its undertakings and act as if it were dead. If the left eye were to concentrate on things of this outer world (that is to say, be absorbed by time and created beings), it would hinder the musing of the right eye.[37]

Chapter 8

People ask: While still in the body could the soul possibly attain some insight into eternity and thereby have a foretaste of eternal life and eternal bliss?

The answer given is generally no. In one sense this is a proper answer. For as long as the soul has its gaze on bodily and temporal things, on created objects, and is consequently filled with images of this varied world, eternal life cannot be grasped.

If the soul is to gaze or look into eternity,[38] it must become chastened[39] and empty of images[40] and detached from all created things and, above all, from the claims of self.

This is the reason some hold that eternity cannot possibly be grasped in a temporal existence.

However, Saint Dionysius considers it possible.[41] This conclusion can be drawn from his words to Timothy: "As far as beholding a divine mystery is concerned, you have to be detached from the sensual and from sensuality and all that the senses can grasp and reason may comprehend and know, including both created and uncreated things. Then you rise in a going-out of yourself, unconscious of the sense-bound and the reason-founded and move into union with that which is above all human existence and knowledge."[42]

Now, if he did not regard such a movement as possible in our temporal existence, why should he have taught it and accordingly given advice to a co-pilgrim on earth?

Besides, you should note that a master speaks about this work of Dionysius's to the effect that the experience is indeed possible and that it may well occur so often in a person's life that he becomes accustomed to looking into and seeing eternity whenever he so desires.[43]

And the glance is like no other.[44] It is nobler, dearer to God, and worthier than anything that the creature can do as creature.[45]

Chapter 9

We should note and know what is the simple truth, namely that no virtue and no good action, not even the confession that God is good, can make man and his soul virtuous, good, or blissful so long as it occurs outside the soul.[46]

Conversely, the same applies to sin and wickedness.[47] It may be commendable to ask, hear about, and gather information concerning good and holy persons, what they have done and suffered, or how they have lived and how God has worked and willed in and through them.[48]

But it is a hundredfold better that man deeply within himself learns and understands the what and the how of his life, what God is working and doing in him and how God wishes to use him and not to use him.[49]

Thus the saying is still true: No outgoing was ever so good that a remaining within was not better.[50]

It should also be pointed out that eternal bliss is rooted in God alone and nothing else. And if man and his soul are to be saved, this one and only God must be in the soul.[51]

You may ask: "What is that one thing?" I answer: "It is Goodness or that which comes through to us as Goodness." It is neither this nor that particular good that we may name, know, or manifest but is all good things and that which is above all good things.[52]

This eternal Good does not have to come into the soul, for It is already there, albeit unrecognized.

When we say that we should come into the One or that the One should come into the soul, it is the same as saying that we should seek, feel, and taste it. Since it is *one*, it follows that unity and singleness is to be preferred to the manifold.

For bliss or blessedness does not come from the wealth of things but from the One and Oneness.[53]

In other words, bliss or blessedness does not depend on any one created thing or on a creature's work but only on God and His works.

Therefore, I should only wait for God and His work and leave aside all creatures with all their works, first of all my own self.

Let me also say this: No great works and wonders God has ever wrought or shall ever do in or through His created world, not even God Himself in His goodness, will make me blessed if they remain outside of me. For blessedness is only present to the extent to which it is within me, as a happening, as an inner knowledge, as love, as feeling and taste.

Chapter 10

Mark this: Illumined people, living in the true light,[54] perceive that everything they might desire or elect is nothing compared to that which has always been desired or elected by all creatures in the depth of their being.

This realization leads them to let go of all desire and reliance on worldly things, surrendering themselves and all to the eternal Good.[55]

Yet there remains in them a desire to advance toward and to get closer to the eternal Good, by a deeper knowledge, a more burning love, a greater preparedness and more complete surrender, and a fuller obedience—and this in such a manner that each illumined person would say: "Would that I were united with the eternal Good as the hand is part of the body."

The illumined always fear that they are not up to the task. They also wish blessedness for all. But they are not bound to this desire and they do not count it as their achievement. They know full well that their desire does not issue from man but from the eternal Good.

No one should claim for himself, as his own, anything that is good, seeing that it belongs only to the eternal Good.

The illumined ones live in freedom. This means that they are free from fear of pain or hell. They have abandoned hope of reward or heaven. They live in pure surrender and obedience to the eternal Good, in love that frees.

This mind dwelled in Christ most perfectly, and it dwells in His disciples, in some more than in others.

It is sad to think that the eternal Good beckons and calls us to the noblest and that we do not want it.

What is nobler than true spiritual poverty? Yet, when it is held up before us we want no part of it.

We wish to be stroked, as it were; there is in us a strong longing for pleasure and sweetness and enjoyment and in the very experience of it we believe that all is well and that we love God.

Yet, when the illusion is withdrawn, we become sore distressed, forget God, and imagine that all is lost.

This is a great breach and a bad sign.

A true lover of God loves Him or the eternal Good equally well in having or not having, in wealth or in want, in sweetness or in bitterness.

May everyone search himself in this regard.[56]

Chapter 11

Christ's soul had to visit hell before it came to heaven.[57]

This is also the path for man's soul.

But note in what manner this occurs as far as we are concerned.

When a person comes to know and see himself he discovers that he is wicked and unworthy of the goodness and comfort that he has received from God or from fellow beings. He then feels that he is damned and lost and unworthy even of that. Yes, he thinks that he is unworthy of the sufferings that he may undergo in his earthly life. He thinks that it is mete and right that all creatures should turn against him and cause him suffering and agony and that he is unworthy of this, too.

He also deems it right that he should be eternally damned and be a footstool for all the devils in hell and, again, that he is unworthy even of that.

He cannot or does not want to ask for comfort or deliverance from either God or man. Rather, he wants to remain uncomforted and unsaved and he does not regret his damnation and his suffering since he judges them mete and just and not contrary to God but in accordance with the will of God. In his view this is right; he is resigned to it.

Only his guilt and wickedness make for grief in his heart. For his guilt and his wickedness are not right, they are contrary to God. Hence this gives him pain and troubles his spirit.

It is this that we call true contrition over sin.[58]

In this way we can say that he who in this present, earthly time enters hell, enters heaven in the afterlife.

He has a foretaste of heaven in this present time. It exceeds all delight and joy that ever was or might be in the temporal, among earthly things.

While the person is thus in hell, no one can comfort him, neither God nor man. It is written: "There is no deliverance in hell."

Someone commented on this as follows: "Let me perish, let me die, comfortless I live, outwardly and inwardly I am condemned, let no one pray that I may be saved."[59]

Now God does not leave man in this hell. No, He takes him to Himself and the result is that man does not ask for anything but the eternal Good alone and knows that the eternal Good is exceedingly precious. Yes, it becomes his ecstasy, his peace, his joy, his rest, his fullness.[60]

And when man asks for and demands nought but the eternal Good, and nothing for himself, then he comes into possession of the eternal Good and knows peace, joy, ecstasy, delight, and such. Thus man is in the kingdom of heaven.

This experience of hell and heaven is like two trustworthy paths for man in his earthly life and happy is the person who travels on them properly and well.

For finally hell departs but the kingdom of heaven will remain.[61]

It is important to note again that when a person is in

this hell, nothing can comfort him and he cannot believe that he will ever be delivered or comforted.

But when he is in heaven nothing can trouble or overwhelm him. He cannot understand how anything could trouble or discomfit him.

In fact, however, just as he was comforted and saved after hell, he may be troubled and overwhelmed after heaven.

When this hell and this heaven enter a person's life he does not know from where. Of himself man cannot, by action or passivity, do anything about their coming or going. Man is unable to surrender to or rid himself of them, create or destroy them. No, the hellish and the heavenly states come and go in accordance with the word, "The wind blows where it will and you hear the sound of it (meaning that it is present) but you do not know whence it comes or whither it goes."[62]

When a person is in one of these two conditions he is on the right road. He can be as safe in hell as in heaven. As long as man is on earth, in a temporal state, he might pass frequently from one to the other, indeed perhaps even during a single day or a single night—and without his own doing.

But when man is in neither of these conditions, he clings too closely to created beings and wavers hither and thither and knows not what he is doing. He should therefore never forget the two roads in his heart.

Chapter 12

Many say that they lack peace and calm. They experience many reverses, much anguish, strain, and suffering.

Now, the person who wants to face and consider this problem truthfully realizes that, if peace were to be had in external things, the devil himself would have peace when

74

everything goes according to his will and pleasure. But he does not.[63]

So we should note and observe the kind of peace Christ left for His disciples in His parting days. He spoke to them and said: "My peace I give to you; not as the world gives do I give to you."[64] For the world's gifts are treacherous.

What kind of peace does Christ mean? He means the inner peace that comes in the midst of hardship, distress, much anguish and misfortune, strain, misery, disgrace, and whatever setbacks there are. Through this peace we become cheerful and patient amid tribulations, just as Christ's dear disciples were—and not they alone but all chosen friends of God and true Christ-followers.[65]

Mark and observe that he who devotes love, diligence, and seriousness to this may well know the true eternal peace that is then the same as God, or as much of God as the creature can possibly receive.[66]

Tauler says: "There are people in our day and age who prematurely abandon external symbols, before the truth of the matter frees them from this kind of dependence."[67]

Because they sever links with such symbols on their own, they are hard put ever to attain truth.

We should always give heed diligently to the works of God and His commands, promptings, and admonitions and distinguish them from human works and purely human commands and admonitions.

Now note that no one can be illumined before becoming purified, chastened, and liberated.

By the same token no one can become united with God if he has not before been illumined. That is what the three stages are for. First comes the purification, second the illumination, and third the union.[68]

Chapter 13

Everything that perished and died in Adam was raised again and made alive in Christ.

And everything that was raised and made alive in Adam perished and died in Christ.

What did this and does this mean?

I answer: true obedience and disobedience.

What, then, is true obedience?

I answer: Man must put aside all "selfdom" and concern with the "Self"[69] so that he does not look out for himself at all, indeed as though he did not exist.

In other words, he should be concerned with his own self as little and think about his own self and his own as little as though he did not exist; yes, he should take as little account of himself as though he were not.

He should view all created things from the same point of view.

What is real, then, and what should one hold on to?

I answer: one thing alone, namely that which we call God. Therein is verily true obedience. That is the true state of affairs in the blessed Eternity. In the Eternal, nothing is sought, contemplated or loved but this one thing only, obedience to God. One considers as nought everything but this one thing.

Now it becomes clear what disobedience is: Man considers himself to be something and believes that he knows and is capable of something, seeks his own interest in the things around himself, is filled with self-love and the like.

Man was and is created for true obedience and owes that obedience to God.

This obedience perished and died in Adam and was raised again and restored in Christ.

Disobedience was raised and made alive with Adam. It died with Christ. Yes, Christ's humanity stood wholly free from the self, more than with any other human. Christ's humanity was nothing but a house or a habitation for God.[70]

His humanity belonged to God. It was a habitation for divinity but did not claim this as its own glory.

Moreover, His humanity did not claim divinity for itself, although it was a habitation for divinity. Nor did it count as a prey anything that this divinity intended, did, or suffered to occur, anything that ever happened and had to be endured in this human form.[71]

No, in Christ's human nature there was no such usurping, not even a hankering or a desire for it. There was only a hankering and a desire to the end that the Divine would receive its due. Christ did not even regard this latter desire as His own.

No more can here be written or uttered about the mind of Christ. It is beyond description. It has never been completely expressed with earthly words. It never will. For the mind of Christ can be described only by Him who *is* this mind and *knows* its ground.[72]

Chapter 14

One speaks of "the old man" and of "the new man." You should know what that language means.

The old man is Adam, disobedience, self, I, and the like.

But the new man is Christ and obedience.

When one speaks of dying and destroying and things like that, one means that the old man should come to nought. And when and where that happens in a true divine light, the new man is born again.

One also says that man should die to himself, that is to say, man's self and his I[73] must die.

Saint Paul speaks of the same thing: Put off the old

man with its practices and put on the new man whom God has created and formed.[74]

He who lives in his selfdom and according to the values of the old man is called—and is—Adam's child.

He may be leading the Adamic life on the fringe or be in the thick of it—he is nevertheless the devil's child and brother.

But he who lives in obedience, the life of the new man, is Christ's brother and God's child.

Lo, where the old man dies and the new one is born again, there the second birth takes place about which Christ says: For unless you are born again and thus renewed you will not come into the kingdom of God.[75]

Saint Paul also says: "For as in Adam all die, so also in Christ shall all be made alive."

This says as much: All who follow Adam in disobedience are dead and will never come alive except in Christ, that is to say, in obedience.

For this reason, as long as man is Adam, or his child, he exists without God.

Christ says: "He who is not with me is against me."[76]

Now, he who is against God is dead before God.

It follows that all the children of Adam are dead before God.

But the one who is with Christ, in obedience, is with God and lives.

I have described sin as a turning away of the creature from the Creator.[77] This accords with what we are saying here. For he who is in disobedience is in sin.

And sin can never be atoned or healed except through a return to obedience.

For so long as man abides in the state of disobedience, sin is never atoned or amended, do what he may. Yes, note this: Disobedience itself is sin.

But when disobedience turns into true obedience, everything is amended, and atoned, and forgiven. There is no other way. Mark this.

If the devil would come to true obedience he would turn into an angel and all his sin and wickedness would be amended and atoned and all at once forgiven.

And if an angel slipped into disobedience, he would right away become a devil even though he did not add hurt to injury.

Would it be possible for a human to live, as a whole and entirely cleansed being, without attachment to his lower self, in renunciation of the entire objective world, in full true obedience? Could a person in that way be without sin and one with Christ?[78]

By means of grace this human being would thus become what Christ is by means of nature.[79]

One contends this cannot be. In the same vein we are reminded: No one is without sin.[80]

Be that as it may, it is in any case a fact that the closer one comes to this obedience, the less is the power of sin; and the farther away one is, the stronger is the hold of sin.

In a word, whether man is good, better, or best of all, whether he is bad, worse, or worst of all, sinful or saved before God, all of this hangs on the matter of obedience and disobedience.

Against this background it has been written· The more of self and I,[81] the more sin and wickedness; the less of self and I the less of sin. It has also been written: The more Mine and I, that is to say I-attachment and selfishness, recede, the more God's I, that is God Himself, increases in me.

If all mankind lived in obedience we would have no pain, no suffering—except of course more bearable bodily suffering of which we should not complain.[82]

If this were the case, all people would be at one, no one would cause his neighbor pain, or suffering. No one would lead his life or do any deed contrary to God. Under those circumstances, from where would pain and suffering come?

But, alas, all humans, the whole world, live in disobedience.

If someone were genuinely and wholly obedient (as we believe that Christ was, else he would not be Christ), all human disobedience around him would be a source of inner, bitter suffering to such a person.

All disobedience is nothing but resistance to God.

Truly, God is not set against any created thing, nor against any works that creatures perform, nor against anything whatever that we can name or think; none of this is contrary to God, it is not displeasing to God. Only one thing is displeasing to God: disobedience and disobedient man.

In short, everything in this earthly life is pleasing to God; He likes it well. Only disobedience and the disobedient please Him not at all. The disobedient person goes wholly against the divine grain and God sorrows much over his disobedience.

The person who experiences in his own suffering and feeling that disobedience is a source of sorrowing for God and that it is against God would rather suffer a hundred deaths, vicariously, in order for disobedience to die, even if it were in just one single soul, and for obedience to be born again.[83]

I grant you, then, that no one lives totally and purely in this obedience, the way Christ did. It is, however, possible for man to approach and come so close to it that he can be called—and can in fact be—godly and divinized.[84]

And the closer man approaches divine obedience and the more godly and divinized he becomes, the more he will feel the pain over disobedience, sin, and unrighteousness, and the more such waywardness will hurt him and the more keenly he will suffer.

Chapter 15

But, say some, there are many who imagine and claim they have died completely to self and become detached from it. They assert that they have reached a stage where suffering does not touch them and they are moved by nothing. It sounds from their account as though each and every one were practicing the kind of obedience we have been talking about and as though no imperfect creatures existed.

These detached folk claim to lead a good undisturbed life and to be of even mind; they feel that all is quite well with the world, whatever happens around them.

No, they are indeed in error. The case is rather as described farther back in this book. It might have been the way these detached ones imagine, had all men accepted obedience. But they have not and therefore the aloofness on the part of some is uncalled for.

Now, one might retort: But man should ideally stand free from all things and claim for himself neither good nor bad.

I answer: No one ought to claim the Good for himself since it belongs to God and God's goodness.

But thanks be to God for the person who is equipped and ready and willing to be a house and a habitation for the Eternal Good and the Godhead. May eternal reward and blessedness be his, so that the Eternal Good and Godhead may channel their power, will, and worth through him unimpeded.

But it is a different matter if one wants to excuse oneself by lifting oneself out of the context of evil and by unloading all guilt onto the devil and wickedness in general.[85]

I declare: Ingratitude, shame, perennial misfortune, and damnation are in store for the one who is equipped and prepared and open to let the devil, untruth, lies, or prevarication and other kinds of wickedness have their way and work in him and become their house and habitation.

Chapter 16

It is important to note, believe, and know that no life on this earth was as noble, good, and dear to God as the life of Christ but that it was at the same time most bitter to human nature and self.

The opposite kind of life, the careless, free life,[86] is most sweet and most pleasant to nature, self, and the I. But it is not the best and the noblest. In many people it becomes the extreme of wickedness.

Although Christ's life was the most bitter of all, it is paradoxically the dearest.

But note that this can be said only from within a knowledge that opens up to true, harmless goodness.[87] Goodness is not this or the other particular thing. It is rather that of which Saint Paul spoke: "When perfection and wholeness comes, all division and imperfection will wane."[88]

This means that wholeness and perfection supersede all that appears in part and that all fragments and all imperfect things are nothing when compared with the perfect Whole.

All knowledge limited to separate parts will come to nought when the Whole is perceived.

When the Whole and the Good are known, one cannot help but long for It and love It. This leads to the disappearance of that other love by which man is fondly attached only to himself and the things of the world.

This inner knowledge also has an eye for the best and the noblest in all created things and lovingly embraces it within the one true Good and for no other reason than for the sake of the true Good.

So you see now what the inner knowledge is: We thereby know that the Christ life is the best and noblest of all lives. And from there it also becomes clear that it is so abundantly precious that we receive and endure it and never ask or worry whether it might help or harm the natural course of things or this and that person and whether it is sweetness or pain.

Let us add that when this true Good is known in a person, Christ's life is also sure to be there and remain to the death of the body.

He who argues differently is in error and he who speaks otherwise lies.

The person in whom Christ's life is not, in him the true Good and the Truth have never been known.

Chapter 17

Let no one believe that he can come to this true Light and this inner knowledge or to the Christ life with the aid of much questioning or secondhand information or by way of reading and studying, or with high skills and academic mastery, or with high natural reasoning.[89]

Moreover, I would say this: As long as a person attaches high regard to something or treats something with preference in his love, opinion, desire, or urge—things of the varied world, that is, his own self or whatever—he will not attain.[90]

Christ Himself spoke about this. He says: If you want to come to Me, then renounce yourself and follow after Me. And he who does not renounce his self and all and leaves and loses it, he is not worthy of Me, nor may he be My disciple.[91]

This means: He who does not let go of and relinquish the things of the world can never truly know nor come into My life.

Should this never have been uttered by a human

voice, the truth of it speaks nevertheless by its own force, for it is thus in true reality.

But as long as man loves the parts, the fragments, and before all himself, and consorts with them and considers this all-important, he is and will remain so blind as to know nothing about the Good.

For he considers as best and dearest what is most useful, comfortable, and enjoyable to himself and to his own.

Chapter 18

Since the life of Christ is most bitter to all natural life, to the self, and to the I—for in the true life of Christ the self and the I and the natural life are surrendered, lost, and given up for dead—natural man shudders as he faces it and he regards it as evil and unjust and foolish. Natural man therefore develops a style that appears to it pleasant and enjoyable and in his blindness he maintains and imagines that this life is the best possible.

Now, to the natural man no life is as comfortable and enjoyable as a free, careless life. So natural man holds on to it and extracts pleasure from his self, his selfhood, his own kind of peace, his own doings, and all that belongs to the self.

This happens most of all where high natural reasoning holds sway, for it climbs so high in its own light and in itself that it fancies itself to be the eternal true light and passes itself off as precisely that.

But this high and learned natural reason deceives itself and pulls with it in the same deceit others who do not know any better and are also inclined in that direction.

Chapter 19

Someone may ask: What is the state of a person who follows the true Light to the best of his ability?

I must tell you frankly that it can never be fully described.

For he who is not on this path is unable to put it in words. And he who is on the path and knows is equally unable to voice it.

Whoever wants to know must wait until he becomes what he knows.

Yet I believe that moral deportment and commands are part of the matter in the following way.

The obligations and rules of this earthly life must be in keeping with and an outflow of the true Light.

But that which does not represent such a "must" or such an "ought" but rather flows from sheer egotistic desire cannot be in keeping with the true Light.

Man often invents for himself many musts and oughts that are actually false.

When he is driven by his pride, avarice, and other vices and also evils of commission and omission, he declares: "It must be, it ought to be."

When he is driven by the urge for people's approval and friendship, or by his body's desire in this direction or that, he declares: "It must be, it ought to be."

Look, all this is false.

If man had no other must and ought than that which God and the Truth inspire in him, he would often have more truly upbuilding tasks than he has right now.[92]

Chapter 20

It is said that the devil sometimes obsesses a person[93] and keeps him in his hold and does so in such a way that the victim is unaware of what the devil does through him or suffers him to do.

The victim is not in his own power but the evil spirit has command over him; he acts and withdraws from action in, with, and through the obsessed at will.

In one sense it is true that the whole world is obsessed and possessed by the devil. To put it differently: The world is filled with lies, falsehood, and other wickedness and vice. That is all the devil.

But obsession and possession should also be understood in a different sense. Let us imagine a person who is obsessed and held by God's spirit to such a degree that he is unaware of the flow and ebb from God and thus does not act in his own power. The power of God then directs at will that person's works, deeds, and leisure. He would be one of those about whom Saint Paul speaks: Those who are guided and led by God's spirit are God's children and are not under law.[94]

Christ spoke about such a person: "For it is not you who speak, but the Spirit of your Father speaking through you."[95]

But I fear that for one who is obsessed with the spirit of God there are a hundred thousand or, rather, innumerable beings obsessed by the devil.

This stems from the fact that people are more like the devil than like God.

The concerns of the I and the self are the devil's field. That is why he is a devil.

My many words on the subject can be summed up by a few: Cut off your self, cleanly and utterly.

But my rather numerous words serve to clarify,

prove, and make distinctions a little more, making it all better understood, I hope.

One may retort: "I am not prepared for anything of this, hence it cannot happen to me." That is the way to invent an excuse.[96]

I would like to answer as follows: If man is not prepared and will not be prepared, it is his own fault.

If man were, in all his thinking and striving, single-mindedly bent on a preparation,[97] how to become prepared, then God would indeed prepare him.[98]

For God devotes as much zeal and love and earnest resolve to preparing man as He does to the pouring out of the Spirit once man is prepared.[99]

But several initiatives have to be taken by man, in accordance with the dictum: "To learn a new art four things are needful."

Needed in the first place is keen yearning for, diligence in, and steadfast resolve about the way to prepare for the Lord. Let us add that nothing ever happens where such yearning is absent.

Second, you should have an example to learn from.

Third, you must constantly and intently look to your Master, and see to it that you believe, obey, and follow Him.

Fourth, you should set about the work and practice it.

If one of these four breaks down, the art will never be learned and mastered.

This is precisely the case with the preparation.

He who has the first, namely diligence and steadfast, determined yearning toward that end, will seek and find all that belongs to, serves, and leads to salvation.[100]

But he who does not have resolve and love and yearning will not seek. Thus he will not find but will remain unprepared and never attain the end.

Chapter 21

We are told about other ways of preparation. One says we should submit to God, in obedience, in carefree serenity[101] and subjection.

This is true of the person who reaches the kind of fulfillment that can be had and attained in this temporal world; that person would have attained the goal in real perfection.

But having said this we may forget that if we are to yield to God in such stillness we must at the same time be subject to everything, including not only God but also ourselves and all created beings, nothing barred.[102]

If you want to be obedient, serene, and submissive to God, you must also be serene, obedient, and submissive in relation to the created world around you, in a spirit of compassionate yielding, and not in a spirit of busyness.

And all this the soul does in silence, resting in its ground and in a secret, hidden, suffering empathy, enabling it to carry all, to suffer with all.

In and during it all that soul takes no recourse to evasion, excuse, resistance, or vengefulness.

The newborn soul rather speaks through it all in loving, humble, true compassion: "Father, forgive them; for they know not what they do."[103] .

This would be a good path to that which is best for us and a preparation for the highest goal that man can attain within time. That goal is the precious life of Christ.

For the paths mentioned above were followed perfectly and wholly in the life of Christ until the end of His bodily life on earth.

There is consequently no better path or preparation to the dear life of Jesus Christ than that selfsame life and its practice to the extent possible.

What belongs to such practice we have touched on a

little in the foregoing. All that has been said here and else-where about the way is a description of a road, or road signs, to the true end.

But no one knows how to say anything about what the true end is.

Yet, he who would like to know may he walk the right path toward it, namely Christ's life.[104]

Chapter 22[105]

We have said there are several ways to Christ's life, by which God and man are joined in such manner that we may in truth claim and know that God and man are one. This oneness unites true perfect God and true perfect man. Yet man makes room for God so that God Himself is there, as man, but also right there Himself, as God.[106]

There is constant interaction in this oneness, both in active deeds and passive serenity, with no part played by the I, and the Me, and the Mine, and such like. You see, in this is true Christ and nowhere else.

Since we have here true perfect man, there is also perfect feeling and perception of joy and sorrow, love and pain, and all that can be felt and experienced, outwardly and inwardly.

Seeing that God *is* that person, we can also say that God experiences and knows love and pain and the like, just as a person who is not God feels and knows all that gives human beings pleasure or pain, but especially per-haps everything untoward.

When God and man become one—meaning that God does His work in man—everything contrary to God and man is keenly felt and experienced.[107]

As man is reduced to nothing in that unity and God becomes all, things that have been a suffering to his natu-ral being are diminished to nothing. On the other hand, what goes against the grain of the Divine and is God's suffering inside the created order will remain as part of God's presence as long as bodily and mental life lasts.

Moreover, the One being in which God and man are united stands on its own and is free from all beings and all things. That is to say, it lives in this freedom thanks to God, not thanks to anything created. For it is a characteristic of God to be detached from the world of things, without self and I.[108] God has no peers.

But it is characteristic of created beings and the natural order that they seek, in all they commit and omit, wherever, the advancement of self and the concerns of self. When a person surrenders and abandons his own self, God enters with His own, that is His self.

Chapter 23

Now, suppose someone has walked in all the ways that beckon him toward the truth and has practiced them. Then the endeavor goes sour for him. When the seeker thinks that all is accomplished, that the death to the world has occurred, that the surrender of the self has conclusively happened—and that he is in God's serenity—as long as and as much as these thoughts are entertained, the devil sows his seed in them.

Two fruits grow out of such seed. One is the feeling of spiritual wealth or rather spiritual pride. The other is undisciplined false freedom.[109] They are like two sisters who stay close together.

Now, this is what emerges. The devil puffs people up into believing and fancying that they have attained the highest and the innermost. The saint, says the devil, is henceforth not in need of Scripture, nor any other support and so on and so forth. In fact, he is supposed to be in need of nothing at all.

From this state of mind arises a sort of peace in him and a self-satisfaction that leads him to declare: "Yes, now I am above all mankind and I know and understand more than the whole world taken together. It is therefore only fair and proper that I act as god for all created things and that all creatures, especially all humans, should serve me, wait on me, and be subservient to me."

So this person then seeks and demands that kind of consideration and accepts it gladly from all created beings, again especially from humans. He considers himself worthy of it. All other people are regarded as donkeys or cattle. Everything that benefits his body, his flesh, his natural needs, and enhances pleasure, pastime, and mirth—the deluded saint thinks he has earned it all and seeks and accepts it whenever the opportunity presents itself. He believes that whatever might be done for him is far too little and that he has deserved whatever good thing comes his way. And all the people that cater to him and serve him are described as faithful hearts, that love and abide in truth, mindful of the poor. Yet, they may even be thieves and murderers. The deluded saint praises them nevertheless. He seeks them out and follows them wherever they are.

But he who does not act according to the will of such proud persons and does not wait on them and does not defer to them, he is unloved by them, reprimanded, and unsought even though he might be as holy as Saint Peter.

Since this overgrown spiritual pride includes the belief that Scripture or doctrine is not essential, the proud ones consider as nought all the rules, orders, laws, and sacraments of the Holy Church; yes, it makes a mockery of them and of all who observe and revere these supports.

One sees here clearly that these two sisters live under the same roof.

Since the inordinately proud imagine that they know

and understand more than all other humans, they jabber more than all others and insist that their words and speech are the only wisdom worth consideration; all other words and speech they declare incorrect, make them targets for scorn, and describe them as folly.

Chapter 24

But the poor of spirit and the spiritually humble are vastly different from those we have just spoken about.[110] For poorness of spirit comes from the discovery and knowledge of true faith, namely that man is nothing in and of himself and on the strength of his own endowments. He is impotent and unfit for anything but infirmity, vice, and wickedness.

From this knowledge it follows that man finds himself utterly unworthy of all that has or will come his way from God or God's creation and that he is a debtor to God and, as God's deputy, to all created beings. So he becomes both compassionate and active in practical service.[111]

Therefore, you have in truth nothing by right. Here one speaks from within a humble mind set: "It would only be fair and right if God and all creatures were against me and had a claim on me; it would also be proper for me to be against no one and to see that I do not have a right to anything."[112]

It follows that such a person does not dare or wish to ask for or desire anything, either from God or from created beings, except the necessities of life—and even in that case only fearfully, for the sake of grace rather than right.

He does not care for his body and his impulses beyond natural necessities. He does not permit anyone to serve him except in necessities—and always in fear and trembling. For he has no right to anything and he considers himself unworthy. This person believes that all his words and discourses are nothing and a folly.

Hence he does not speak to a fellow being in order to teach or to upbraid him, except when prompted by godly love and faithfulness—and even then fearfully and most lovingly.

In this spiritual poverty and humility one finds and understands that all humans are bent upon and turned toward the self, evil practices, and wickedness. One also sees that because of this inclination, it becomes necessary and useful to have order, rules, law, and commands. Law and command make our blindness[113] evident to us and constrain wickedness into order.

Were it not for this, people would be much more wicked and undisciplined than dogs and cattle. Many a person was drawn and turned to the truth through outward rules and order; without them it would not have happened.

Also, few people come to the truth who have not begun with the practice of order and rules; after all, they did not know anything different or better. Therefore, laws and commands, order and rules, are not to be despised and scorned in the realm of humble spirituality and spiritual poorness nor should those persons be despised who observe and follow them. Such persons pray in loving pity, lamentation, and compassion: "God and Truth, we lament, and You lament with our soul, that human blindness, infirmity and wickedness render some things needful and ordained that in reality are not needed, nor should have to be ordained."

The rules are an appeal to those who do not know any better, to come to the truth so that they may know and inwardly recognize the reason for all laws and all order.

Those who know take up the task among those who

know no better, and practice with them. The first intention is that they abide by the rules and not turn to wicked things. But then the hope is also that they may be brought closer to the kingdom.

Everything submitted here concerning poverty and humility is truly the way we have said. It is testified and proven by the life of Christ and His words. For He carried out and completed all the works of true humility. One finds this in His life and in His words: "Learn from me; for I am gentle and lowly in heart, and you will find rest for your soul."[114]

He did not neglect or despise the covenant[115] and the law, nor the people who lived under the covenant.[116] But, He said, keeping them is not enough; one should forge ahead into the real truth.[117]

Saint Paul writes: Christ took the covenant upon Himself to redeem those who were under the covenant. He means that Christ wants to bring them to something closer and better.[118] The Lord also said: "The Son of Man came not to be served but to serve."[119] In short, let me repeat: In Christ's words and works and life we find nothing but sheer humility and poverty.[120] Wherever God has become man[121] and Christ is consequently present, this outcome must needs follow. But where pride develops and false spiritual wealth and the undisciplined, free mind, there Christ is not, nor His true follower.

Christ said: "My soul is very sorrowful, even to death." He means the bodily death, and thinks of the whole time from His birth of Mary until the death of the body and what that sorrow was like we have already talked about.[122]

Christ furthermore says this: "Blessed are the poor in spirit." This word speaks of the truly humble. "For theirs is the kingdom of heaven."[123]

Truth also speaks about the opposite, although we do

not find it literally in the Holy Writ: Unblest and accursed are the spiritually wealthy and proud, for theirs is the kingdom of the devil.[124]

So we certainly know at what point God takes over in man.[125] Wherever Christ and His true followers are, we are sure to find deep humility and poverty of spirit and a chastised and reflective mind. In this mood there is bound to be a secret, hidden sorrow and suffering lasting into bodily death.

He who fancies something else about life in God has been deceived. He also deceives others along with himself, I repeat.

Nature and self recoil from the life-in-God and hold to the life of false lawless freedom, as I also said. Now, aided by such natural reluctance an Adam or a devil appears on the scene, armed with a subterfuge: "You are almost saying that Christ became void of His own self and everything connected with it. Yet He often spoke of His self and glorified His self in one way or another."

Answer: Where Truth is active in deed and in will, her will and desire and work revolve around just one thing: that she may become known and manifest.[126]

This was the truth in Christ; both word and work were parts of it. But the best and most profitable of it all is this: He was free from these word and work events, just as free as He was from other things around Him, in the sense that He never claimed them as His own.

But you say: "So there was after all a 'wherefore,' an ulterior motive, in Christ?"

I answer: You ask the sun, "Why do you shine?" She says, "I have to shine and can do nothing else. It is my nature. It is in me to shine. But I am at the same time free from this nature and from the shining for I do not emit my own light."

This is the way it is with God and Christ and all that

is godly and belongs to God. It wills, works, desires, nothing but the Good, for the sake of the Good. There is no other "wherefore."

Chapter 25[127]

Moreover, let us point to the following. When it is said—indeed, Christ Himself says it—that man must forsake and surrender all things, this should not be understood to mean that there is nothing for us to do and to take in hand.[128]

For man is also meant to be a doer and carry out ordinary tasks as long as he lives. This, however, should not be perceived in such a way that the union with God depends on man's creaturely power, his activity, his repose, and his learning.

What is then this union? Nothing but a truly pure simple repose in the one eternal Will of God. Or—it can also be expressed this way—the union is to be without will so that the created will flows into the eternal Will and ceases to be therein, becomes nought, with the result that the eternal Will alone wills, works, and speaks in us.

Now mark what serves and aids a person toward this end. Neither words, works, rules, nor a single creature's effort, nor the efforts of all created beings can attain the union. Deeds, learning, abilities, activity, cannot attain it. We must let all such designs go, that is to say, we should not entertain the idea that any kind of works, words, rules, wit, or mastery, briefly, any created things at all, can contribute or be of help here.

Rather, one has to let all this go, leave these things for what they are, and proceed into the union with God. But, of course, the outward things are parts of the design; we must live with them in our action and inaction. To be specific: We must sleep and awaken, walk and stand still, talk and keep silent, and many other things that must be as long as we live.

Chapter 26

Also note this: When true union with God takes place, deep in our being, the inner man is enduringly rooted in that union. But God lets the outer man be moved every which way, in and to matters that are and occur by the rules of earthly life.

This expresses itself in such a way that the outer man says—and, indeed, he is speaking accurately: "I will neither be nor not be, neither live nor die, know nor not know, act nor remain passive, and other such contrary things. But I am prepared in obedience to do what must be and must take place, whether it unfold in inner compassion or in active service."

The outer man has no "wherefore" or real purpose except to fulfill the eternal Will. It becomes truly acknowledged that the inner man shall stand immovable and the outer man must and should be moved. If the inner man has a wherefore in the outer movements of life it is nothing but precisely the duty and obligation ordained by the eternal Will. This is the case where God Himself becomes man, as we see in Christ.

Where man is of this kind and lives from the divine light no spiritual pride appears, no reckless freedom, no undisciplined disposition, only a deep humility and a chastised, reflective, contrite mind.

To this life also belong reputable behavior, rectitude, consistency, truthfulness, and everything else pertaining to virtue in human relations. Such things must be there. Where they are not, something has gone wrong with the union. We spoke more about this elsewhere.

For whereas this or that particular deed or virtue

does not bring about or promote the union, these qualities can, on the other hand, not hinder or obviate it. Only man himself can do this, through his self-will.

Chapter 27

One hears people assert that man can and should become free from suffering during his earthly life in all respects as Christ was after His Resurrection.[129]

They try to prove and establish this by citing Christ: "But after I am raised up, I will go before you to Galilee, there you shall see Me."[130] This statement by Christ is also quoted: "A spirit has not flesh and bones as you see that I have."[131]

These utterances are then interpreted as follows. "As you have seen Me and followed Me as I was in a mortal body and life, so you should also see Me as I go ahead of you and you follow Me into Galilee; this is to say, you will follow Me into a state where pain has gone and serenity reigns; you will taste it, live in it, remain in it before you have gone through and suffered the death of the body. As you see Me appear in a body of flesh and bones, yet beyond suffering, in a similar manner you will also, before your bodily death, become free from suffering and soar beyond pain in your mortal humanity."

I would like to counter these assertions. First, Christ did not mean that man can and should attain that stage unless it were preceded by all the suffering that He, Christ, went through and endured.

Now, Christ did not attain this stage before He had passed through and suffered the death of His body and the experiences that came with it. Thus no man can or should attain that perfect peace and spiritual serenity while mortal and subject to suffering.

For if this state is the noblest and best and if it were possible and spiritually commendable to attain it within our earthly life, then, as pointed out, it would also have occurred in the life of Christ.

For Christ's life was and is the noblest, the best, most pleasing to God, the loveliest of all lives that were lived and ever will be lived.

Yet, since this serene freedom from earthly woe was not permitted and intended to occur in Christ, it will never appear in any human being, for this would mean that a human life would in fact be the best and the noblest.

You are of course free to fancy such a thing and you can, of course, talk about it. But fancy and words do not that freedom make.

Chapter 28

It has been suggested that man is able to transcend virtue, rule, order, command, law, and rectitude in human affairs, to the end that one puts it all aside, throws it off and destroys it.[132]

There is an element of truth in the assertion. But there is also an untruth hidden in it. Let me point out the following: Christ was above the Christ life; He was above all virtue, rule, order, and the like. The devil is also above them, but with a difference.

For Christ stood and stands above all this in the sense that none of His words and works, rules, His action and refraining from action, His silence and His speech, His suffering, indeed nothing that ever took place in Christ emerged out of necessity for Himself; He did not need any of those things; they were of no use to Him personally.

It is the same with all our virtue, order, rectitude, and the like. For what is transcended on account of them—if we actually do transcend anything by them—that is all present in Christ, it is already there in advance.

In this sense it is consequently true that our virtues

should be put aside. In this sense we should also understand Saint Paul when he says: Those who are instructed, prompted, and led by the Spirit of God are God's children and are in a way not under the law.[133]

That means, one does not have to teach them what they should do and what they should omit. For their Master, the Spirit of God, will teach them well.

Also, one does not have to enjoin or command them to do good, shun evil, and the like. For this Master who teaches them what is good and not good and best or less than best, He bids and calls them to abide in the best and leave the rest behind, and Him they obey.

So in this sense they need not look out for instruction or command regarding the law. There is another sense in which they are in no need of law: They do not thereby receive or win something for themselves or in any way gain advantage for themselves.

For whatever influence one might exert on the way everlasting by this method or with assistance, counsel, words, and works from any created being, the liberated ones have it already. Thus in this sense it is true that one may rise above all law and all virtue and also above the works and knowledge and powers of any creature.[134]

Chapter 29[135]

Let us speak about that other assertion, namely that we should reject and do away with the Christ life as well as command and law, rule, and order, and so on, and pay no heed to them, despise them and scoff at them. Now, this is a falsehood and a lie.

No doubt some would say: Since Christ and other humans can obtain or gain nothing by the Christ life or draw spiritual uses from the observance of rules, order, and so on, and when they already have what can be obtained thereby, what further concern is then all this talk of law to them? Should they not let go of it? Should they still deal with, practice, and pursue the Christ life and the commands?[136]

I would like you to look closely at the fact that there are two kinds of light. The one is true, the other is false. The true light is the eternal light, which is the same as God. It also manifests itself as created light, godly or divine, termed grace.[137] All this is true light.

On the other hand, the false light is nature or of nature. Why is the first light true and the second false? You will more readily perceive this by intuition than express it in writing or in speaking.

To God as Godhead[138] we can ascribe neither will, nor knowing, nor manifest revelation, nor any particular thing that can be named, spoken, or conceived by thought.

But it belongs to God as God to revere Himself, to know and to love Himself, to reveal Himself to Himself—and all this still in God, all still in God as being, not as manifested work, for He is still the Godhead without created beings.

It is in this reverence and this revealing that distinction between persons arises.[139]

But when God as God is made man or when God lives in a godly person or in a divinized or sanctified person, there is always something in the human manifestation that is God's own, belongs only to God and not to the created being; it is in God Himself, quite apart from the creature, originally, substantially, not as form or deed. Now, however, God wanted his innermost to be acted out and practiced. What else is the God life for? Should it remain idle? What use would it then be? That which is of no use whatever is also in vain and this is not God's will, nor nature's.

God wants His desire to reveal Himself, to be worked out—and that, if it has to be, cannot be without created beings; yes, if there were no manifested things, no created things, what would or should God Himself be or what is He in that case?[140]

Here we have to halt our steps and turn around else we might go so far and probe so deeply into this question that we would not know where we are or how to find our way out again.[141]

Chapter 30

I will now ask you to think about God from the aspect of the Good. God is Goodness looked upon as Goodness, not this or that particular form of good.

Note this: What exists in a particular spot cannot be in all spots, nor transcend every place where it appeared. What is here today and gone tomorrow does not abide forever, nor does it cover all time. What is particular, a special thing, is not all things, nor does it embrace all things.

You see, if God were a particular thing that we could point to, He would not be all in all and above all—and the latter is of course the case. If He were only in the particular He would not be true Wholeness. Therefore, God is. Yet He is not a special created thing that created beings perceive, name, conceive, or describe in their role as creatures.

So if God-as-Good were a particular good He would not be all Goodness and above all good things. He would not be the One total and perfect Good, which He is.

Now God is also a light and an inner knowing,[142] whose nature is to shed light, to shine and to know, for God is light and knowing; He must emit light and knowing and all this giving and knowing is God, apart from the created world.

It is not there as a manifest activity but as a being or as a beginning. Yet if this being is to express itself as activity, as creative work, this must take place through created beings.

You see, where this inner knowing and this light are at work in a material being, this being recognizes and testifies as to what it is, that it comes from the Good itself, not from this or that particular thing.

Since it is neither this nor that particular thing, its inner knowing and testimony does not spring forth from separate things. Rather, it knows and testifies that there is a true, simple, perfect Good that is not identical with individual good things but is the totality of all good things, that which exceeds separate forms of goodness.

We have said that the Light testifies to the one, simple Good. But what does it say about that one Good?

Mark this: as God is simple goodness, inner knowledge, and light, He is at the same time also one will, love, righteousness, and truth, the innermost of all virtue. Yet, although different, all of these are one being in God and none of the particular goods can ever be realized or practiced in deeds without created beings. For the good in God without creatures is nothing but being and beginning without deeds.[143]

But suppose that the One, who is the All, receives a human being and becomes his strength and brings him to the point of spiritual capability where the One and All can recognize his own in this human life. In that situation will and love, united in the One, are actually proclaimed by Himself in and through the follower, for the One is both light and knowledge. The One, who is the Good, cannot will anything except that which He is.

So, as this person continues on his way, he wills and loves nothing but the good for the sake of the Good, for no other reason but its goodness. He does not will and love because the circumstance is a particular one or because it is good for this or that purpose, pleasure or pain, joy or sorrow, sweetness or bitterness, or similar contrasts. He does not choose to take such questions into consideration, least of all not on behalf of the self or as a self.

For in the life now described all matters of the self and the I and the Me have been surrendered and abandoned. There one does not assert: "I love myself, I love you,[144] I love this or that."

If you were to ask Love, "What do you love?" the answer would be, "I love goodness." "Why?" She replies: "Because it is good and for the sake of goodness."

It is good, right, and well warranted to love in that sense. If something were better than God it should be loved better than God.[145] Therefore God does not love Himself as Himself but as the Good. If there were something better than God, and God knew thereof, He would love it and not Himself.

Thus the temporal I and the self[146] are totally separated from God. They do not belong to God except as He needs them to reveal personhood.

Now, the descriptions above must become reality in a godly or a truly divinized person or else he would not be godly or divinized.

Chapter 31

It follows from what we have said that love in the heart of a divinized person is undefiled and unadulterated, borne by good will toward all humans and all created things. Therefore, from within this purity mankind and all created things must be sincerely loved and one must will and wish and do what is best for them.

People may do what they will to a divinized person, good things or bad, pleasure or pain; yes, if someone killed a divinized person a hundred times over and the victim should come to life again, he would still harbor love for his killer,[147] and this despite the injustice, evil, and wickedness committed; he would wish the assailant well, not begrudge him anything good but desire and ask for it. He would give him the very best, as soon as his assailant is ready to receive and accept it.

This can be seen, proved, and confirmed in Christ's life. For He spoke to Judas who betrayed Him: Friend, why have you come?[148]

It was as if He had said: "You hate Me, you are My foe, but I love you, I am your friend and you wish Me, desire for Me, and do to Me the very worst you can. But I will desire and wish for you the very best and I would give it to you and do it to you, if you were prepared to receive and accept it."

That is just as though God were speaking straight out of His humanity: "I am pure, single-minded Goodness. Thus I cannot will, desire, wish or do anything but good. If I am to react to your evil and your wickedness I have to do it with good since that is all I am and have."

It follows that God in a divinized person does not wish or will to act as an avenger who reacts only to all the evil one has done or will do to Him.

This is evident with Christ, who said: "Father, forgive them; for they know not what they do."[149]

There is also this trait with God that He uses no force with anyone to act or to omit action. Rather, He lets each person do or leave undone, according to that person's will, whether it be good or bad. He resists no one.

Again, we see this in Christ's life. He did not want to resist or defend Himself against evildoers. When Saint Peter wanted to defend Him, He said: Peter, put your sword back; it is not for me and those who are mine violently to resist and defend and bring force to bear.[150]

In the same manner a divinized person does not oppress or distress anyone. Take this to mean that it never enters his will, his desire, or his judgment to act, omit, speak or remain silent with the intention to cause someone pain or distress.

Chapter 32

Some may say: "Since God wills, desires, and does the best for everyone, He should help and act in such a fashion as to fulfill everyone's desires so that one person who wishes would become pope, another one bishop, and so forth."

My answer is this: He who aids a fellow being to realize self-will contributes to the very worst. For the more man follows after and grows in self-will, the further he is from God and the true Good.[151]

Of course, God is most willing to help man toward that which is God's best treasures and hence also best for man among all things.

If this is to happen, all self-will must be done away with, as we said. God would gladly help man toward this. When man seeks his own good, he never actually finds it. For man's highest good would be and truly is that he should not seek and love himself or his own.[152] God teaches and speaks thus: If you want God to help you to the best—and to your own best—you must follow God's work and teaching and command. In this and in no other way will you be helped.

God teaches and admonishes man to forsake himself and all things and to follow Him only.

He who loves his soul, his own self, guarding and saving it—in other words, he who seeks his own in natural things—will lose his soul. But he who is unsolicitous for his own soul and forsakes his self and his own things[153] will keep his soul and save it into eternal life.[154]

Chapter 33

In a divinized person the godly characteristic is humility, deep in a person's being. Where there is no humility we cannot speak of a divinized person. Christ taught this in words, works, and life.

Humility stems from the inner recognition made in the true Light that being, life, knowledge, wisdom, and power are truly rooted in God, not in the created world. The creature is of itself and has from itself nothing. When it turns away from true Goodness in will and work, nothing is left but wickedness.

It is therefore an undeniable truth that the creature as creature is in itself unworthy, has no real claim on anything, no one is indebted to it, neither God nor fellowman. The creature should rightly be surrendered to God's hands, subject to Him. This is the highest and the most important concern in man's life.[155]

What is thus—or should be—turned over into God's hands and subject to God must also be surrendered to all creatures and fellow beings (and, briefly, not in terms of outer activity but in terms of inner compassion). If this does not happen the submission is all false.

From this latter fact, from this article of truth, comes true humility, together with the former article about the allegiance we owe to God. If this were not the truth and the best and highest divine righteousness, Christ would not have taught it in words and fulfilled it in His life.

This is where true reverence is born. In truth this is God's way with us: We must, by the power of divine truth and righteousness, be subject to God and all creatures and no single thing and being should be subject to us.

God and all creatures have a right over and claim on the person who abides in God, but that creature has no right to them. I owe debts to all things, no one owes me anything. The divinized creature accepts this compassionately so that he is called to bear all things from others and, when occasion arises, do all things for others.

Out of this grows that spiritual poverty about which Christ spoke: "Blessed are the poor in spirit, for theirs is the kingdom of heaven."[156] Christ taught this in words and fulfilled it in His life.

Chapter 34

It is important to observe the following. One commonly says that a certain thing is or occurs against God, is contrary to God, provokes God.

But you should know that God has turned against no creature, is provoked by no creature with respect to what it is, how it lives, knows, or acts. Whatever the so-called affront, it certainly does not vex God.

The fact that the devil or man is and lives, that is good and of God.

For God is all this essentially and originally.

He is the being of all beings, the Life of all living things and the Wisdom of all the wise.

All things have their being more truly in God than in themselves and in their own powers, life, and other endowments.[157]

If this were not so, God would not be all-embracing Goodness. Hence we can say that all things are good. What is good is pleasing to God. He wants to have it. It is not contrary to Him.

But what is then contrary to God and pains Him? Nothing but sin. And what is sin but that the creature wills differently from God, defies God? Everyone can see this in himself. For he who wills differently from what I will, contrary to me, is my enemy. The one who wills the way I will is my friend, pleases me. Our relationship to God is similar. Our contrary will is our sin; it gives Him pain and sorrow.

The person who wills differently from myself or contrary to myself in what he does or omits, says or keeps silence about, does all this in contrariness and this is hard to take.

The same is true of God. He who pits his will against God in what he commits or omits, yes in whatever he does, goes against God and therefore commits sin. The will that wills contrary to God is a will set against God's will.

For Christ says: "He who is not with me is against me."[158]

He means: If you do not desire to be with me, if you have not united your will with mine, your will is against me.

Hereby can everyone plainly see if he is without sin, whether or not he does sin; he can see what sin is, how to atone for sin, how it can be amended.

This contrariness to God is called—and is—disobedience.

Adam, I, self, self-will, sin, the old man, the turning away and separation from God—that is all one and the same thing.

Chapter 35

Let us say again: Into God as God no pain, grief, or dislike can come. Yet God is grieved on account of man's sin.

Since grief cannot be in God outside the creature, it occurs when God is in man or in a divinized man.

Sin is such a pain to God, it saddens Him so much, that He would Himself be tortured and bodily die so that He might thereby wipe out a person's sin.

If we asked God if He would rather live so that sin should remain, or die in order to destroy sin, He would choose death.

For God feels more pain over man's sin and it gives Him more grief than His own torture and death.[159]

Now, if one person's sin causes God pain, how much more, then, the sins of all men? So you see how deeply man grieves God with his sins.

Where God is man or in a divinized person one does not grieve over anything but sin. Nothing else gives real pain.

For all that is or occurs without sin, that is what God will have and be.

Yet grief and sorrow over sin should and must remain in a divinized person until he leaves his body in death, even if he were to live until the latter day, or forever.

From this came Christ's hidden anguish of which no one reports or knows but Christ Himself. Therefore we call it what it is: hidden.

This hidden sorrow over man's sinful condition is an attribute of God's that He has chosen and that He is pleased to see in man. But it is God's attribute above all. Sorrow over sin does not finally belong to man; man is not himself capable of it. Wherever God can bring it about in us, it is the most pleasing and most appropriate but at the same time the most bitter and heavy undertaking on which we can enter.

What we have been describing here is one of God's attributes, which he yet would like to see in man. For it is in man that it should be practiced and put into effect. The true Light teaches us about sorrow over sin; it teaches us, moreover, that man, in whom it is put into effect and practiced, should claim that divine mood for himself as little as though he were not there.

For then man recognizes with inner knowledge that he himself would not be capable of creating the awareness of sin and that it does not belong to him.

Chapter 36

Wherever such a divinized person lives, there we have the best, noblest, and, in God's eyes, most valuable life that ever was or can be.

Attachment to this kind of life is rooted in a love of goodness for the sake of the good. It has an eye for the best and noblest in all things for the sake of the good. And it is so deep that it can never be quite abandoned and rejected.

In the case of divine sorrow, the kind we now have described, the person who harbors it cannot possibly get out of its thrall even if he should live to the latter day.

Should you die a thousand deaths and be afflicted by all the misfortunes that might ever befall, you would rather suffer than abandon the noble life. If given an opportunity to exchange your life for that of an angel's, you would not take it.

We have now answered the question: When man can obtain nothing in addition to what he has by virtue of the Christ life and does not seem to have much practical use for it, what further meaning does it have?

The life in Christ is not chosen because one derives use from it or can obtain something thereby but on account of love for its nobility and because it is dear to God and highly rated by Him.

Whoever says he has had enough of it or that he wants to put it aside has never tasted it or come to know it from within. For the person who has in truth felt it or tasted it can never give it up.

Therefore, the person who leads a life in Christ with the intention of obtaining some use or earning some glory from it embraces this life as a hireling who is out for recompense and not from love; he possesses none of Christ's life. He who is not devoted to it out of love has no part of it. He might fancy he has it but he is mistaken.

111

Christ led His life not from expectation of reward but from love. And love makes life light, not heavy, so that it is joyfully led and willingly endured.[160]

But he who does not lead his life from love but fancies it should bring reward, for him the eternal life turns so heavy that he wishes to be promptly rid of it.

It is a sign of a hireling that he wishes his work would soon end.

But a true lover of life in Christ does not take offense at life's work, length, or suffering.

Hence it is written: "To serve and live for God is easy to everyone who does it." This is true of the one who does it from love. But it is hard for the one who does it for reward.

So it is with all virtue and all good works, with order, sincerity, and the like.

Chapter 37

One says—and rightly so—that God is above and without rules, measure, and order, yet renders to all things rules, order, measure, and rectitude.[161]

This should be understood in the following manner.

God wills this ordered life. In Himself, without the created beings, He cannot have that.

For in God, without the relationship to the creature,[162] our human distinctions cannot be made between order and absence of it, rules for living and lack of them, and such things. God, however, has ordained it thus that these structures should be.

For as far as word, work, and deportment are concerned we always stand in a choice between, on the one hand, rule and rectitude or, on the other, disorder.

Now, orderliness and rectitude are better and nobler than the opposite.

Four kinds of people deal with order, command, and rule in four different ways.

Some lead an ordered life neither for God's sake nor out of a particular personal desire, but simply because they are compelled. They do the least possible and it all turns sour and burdensome for them.

Another group observes laws and rules for the sake of reward. That is, people who know nothing beyond this perspective and fancy that one can and will in this and no other way obtain and earn the kingdom of heaven and eternal life. They consider that person holy who observes a great many ordinances and the person who neglects and omits even some little rule as lost to the devil. They show great seriousness, and diligence to boot, yet it all turns sour for them.

The third kind of people are the wicked, false spirits who fancy themselves as perfect, and speak accordingly. They imagine that they are in no need of rule and law and in fact scoff at all talk about order.

Fourth, we have the illumined ones, guided by the true Light. They do not practice the ordered life in expectation of reward. For they do not want to acquire anything with the aid of it, nor do they hope that something will accrue on account of it. No, they do what they do in the ordered life out of love.

They are not so concerned about outcome, how a particular behavior will turn out, how soon, and so on. Their concern is rather that things will work out well, in peace and inner ease. And should perchance something less weighty in the orderly program be neglected, they are not lost in despair.[163]

For they know, of course, that order and rectitude are better and nobler than lack of it. So they wish to keep the rules but they also know that their salvation and bliss do not depend on the observance. Therefore they are not as anxious as the others.

These people are condemned and judged by persons in groups two and three.

For instance, the hirelings or the reward folk say of them that they are too careless and sometimes pronounce them unrighteous and similar accusations.

The group consisting of "the free spirits"[164] scoffs: "They embrace coarse and foolish things."

But the illumined keep to the middle,[165] which is the best.

For a lover of God is better and more pleasing to God than a hundred thousand hirelings. This also applies to their outward actions.

Note that it is the inner man who receives God's law, His word, and all His teachings, describing for him how to become united with God.

Where this happens, the outer man is structured and tutored by the inner man, and learns that no outward law or teaching is needed.

But human laws and commands belong to the outer man. They are needed when one knows nothing better. Else people would not know what to do and what to omit and so become like dogs or cattle.

Chapter 38

I have briefly mentioned the false light. I would like to say something further about what it is and how it works.

Look, all that is contrary to the true Light belongs to the false light.

It is an essential quality of the true Light that It does not know deceit, is not inspired by will to deceive, and that It cannot itself be deceived.

But the false light is deceived and constantly pulls others into its deceit.

God does not wish to deceive anyone. He cannot desire that someone be deceived. This is consequently true also about the true Light.

Note now, that the true Light is God, is divine; the false light is nature or natural.

It is a mark of God that He does not will, seek, or desire a number of special things in a divinized person. He wills and seeks just one thing, goodness as Goodness and only for the sake of the Good.

The same must be said about the true Light.

It is, on the other hand, a mark of a created being that it exists in this or that particularity. It is also typical of created beings that, in their love and work, they always aim for a special gain. The natural creature does not have in mind the Good as simply the Good, for the sake of the Good. It rather thinks of the Good as a particular good that must be attained.

As God is the true Light, void of all I and self[166] and all self-indulgence, so, conversely, the mark of the natural creation and the natural false light is to pamper the I, the Me, and its outgrowths. Nature with its natural false light is marked by the urge to seek itself and its own in all things more than goodness as Goodness. This is simply the characteristic both of the natural order and of each individual creature.

Now note how man's nature is deceived from the beginning. It will not have and does not elect goodness as Goodness, but it wills and elects itself and everything connected with itself as the best. Yet that is a false way and here we have the first and basic deception.

Man fancies himself to be what he is not. He fancies himself to be God, yet he is only nature, a created being. From within that illusion he begins to claim for himself the traits that are the marks of God. He does not claim only what is God's insofar as God becomes man or dwells in a divinized person. No, he claims what is the innermost of God, God's prime mark, namely the uncreated, eternal Being.

We say about God as Godhead that He is free from want, needs nothing, is disengaged, free, above all things, and so on. This is of course true. So are other words about God: that He is unchangeable, not moved by anything, is beyond human knowledge and that all He does is good.

"Look, this is what I, too, want to be," says the false light. "For the more one is made into God's likeness the better one becomes. Yes, I want to be God, sit at the side of God, be like Him." This is precisely what Lucifer, the devil, did.[167]

God in eternity is without pain, suffering, and grief. He is not burdened by nor does He feel pain and grief on account of that which is or happens.

But when God is in human form and present in a divinized person, then we are dealing with something different.

Briefly, it is only this false light that places the veil of deception over things.

Those that are thus perverted can and will be deceived only by the false light, and only created beings, the natural world, and everything that is not God and not divine fall for it. You can therefore say that this light itself is nature and that it is deceived.

Indeed, the false light deceives itself.

You might ask: From where does the fact arise that this light does deceive everything that can be deceived?

It stems from the rest of its clever reasoning. For inside this light there may be such a feeling of wisdom, subtlety, and artfulness that one seems to have risen above and climbed beyond nature, indeed, so far above that nature and creature can never reach this height. The natural light therefore begins to assume it *is* God. It claims all that which is the mark of God, especially what God is in eternity, not what He is as man. The natural or false light asserts and fancies that it stands above all works, words, rules, orders—yes, above the bodily life of Christ, which He lived in His humanity.

The natural false light thus claims to be untouched by all creaturely life, be it evil or good, against God or not—that is immaterial to it. It is not dependent on anything in this world, just like God in eternity. It believes it possesses all the other marks that signify God in eternity, in contradistinction to man. It claims all this for itself: It is worthy of these marks and all creatures should rightfully serve and be subject to it.

So no pain, suffering, or grief remain in relation to anything, except for a bodily and sense-bound experience that must needs continue until the death of the body and the kind of suffering that comes with it.

The person persuaded by the false light says and fancies that he has transcended Christ's bodily life and that one should be free from suffering and unmoved like Christ after His Resurrection. And we could mention many other strange falsehoods that arise from this reasoning.

Since this false light is nature, its characteristic is the natural, that is to say, it loves and seeks itself and its own in all things and that which to nature and itself is most self-indulgent and the most pleasant.

Because it is deceived, it fancies and proclaims as the best that which seems to it most pleasant and most comfortable. It maintains that each person should seek, do, and desire his own best and be concerned only with his own good, in other words, what answers his own fancy.

If someone informs the person of the false light about the one true Good, which is neither this nor that particularity, he knows nothing about it; it is a matter of scorn for him—and no wonder, for nature as nature cannot arrive at this discovery. Since the false light is nature merely, it simply is unable to attain that truth.

The false light falsely proclaims that the conscience and its workings have been transcended and this, it argues, makes right all that is done by its inspiration.

Yes, such a false spirit steeped in this error is reported to have said that if he killed ten humans it would be to him like having killed a dog.

In sum, the deceiving and deceived light shuns all that assails natural man and is a burden to him. This is of course typical for we deal here with nature.

Since, moreover, it is so utterly deceived that it imagines itself to be God, the false light would swear by all that is holy that it truly knows what is the best and that it has reached the best as far as true judgment and genuine desire are concerned.

The false light is therefore never converted and cannot be guided onto the right path. The same can be said of the devil.

One should also note this. To the extent to which this light imagines it is God and claims divinity for itself, it is Lucifer, the devil.

And to the extent to which it rejects the Christ life and other things that belong to true Goodness and that Christ has taught and fulfilled, to that extent the false light becomes an anti-Christ, for it teaches and lives against Christ.

As this light is deceived by its own clever reasoning, it deceives all that are not turned toward God, that is to say all those whom the true Light and its love have not illuminated.

For wherever and whoever those persons may be whom the true light has illuminated, they will never be deceived.

All those in whom the true Light is not are turned

upon themselves[168] and consider their selves as the best, and put first that which appears good and comfortable to them personally.

Whoever gives and presents this to them as the best and aids and teaches them to attain such goals, him they follow, considering him the best of instructors.

This is precisely what the false light teaches. Therefore all those follow it who do not know the true Light and so they are deceived together.

It is predicted about anti-Christ that, when he comes, he who then does not have God's sign follows after him, but he who has that sign does not follow him. There is correspondence here.

True, it is best if what is best for you could be attuned to that which is God's highest Good. But this cannot be while you focus on and love what you consider your own good.

If you are to find and attain your truest good you have to lose your good in order to find it, as has been said before.[169]

If man strives to let go of and lose his own good or best in order that he may find his true good, he is likely to confuse the two. Few can come to God along that road.

The false light maintains that one ought to be without knowledge of sin[170] and that it is foolish and gross to consider it. It tries to prove this point by reference to Christ, for He did not know sin.[171]

We can retort: The devil has likewise no knowledge of sin but he is none the better for it.

Note what knowledge of sin is. It is to know within that man has strayed and will stray from God in his will—that is what we call sin. Man himself is to blame for this, not God. God is innocent of sin.

Who can look on himself as guiltless except for Christ and few besides Him?

He who lacks knowledge of sin is either Christ or the devil.

Briefly: Where the true Light is, there is a true righteous life, pleasing and precious to God.

Although it is not the perfect life of Christ, it is nonetheless formed and righted according to it; the Christ life is loved and what flows from it: rectitude, order, and the rest of the virtues.

Inside this life selfishness, the concerns of the I and the Mine, lose their hold, together with all that belongs to these concerns. Nothing is the object of love or ambition there except the Good for Its own sake and as Good.

But where the false light is present one devotes little attention to the Christ life and the virtues. That which brings comfort and enjoyment to the natural urges is cherished and sought in the false life.[172]

Out of this arises false, undisciplined freedom resulting in careless and reckless living in ordinary life.

The true Light is God's seed grain and brings forth God's fruits.

The false light is the devil's seed grain and when it is sown, the devil's fruits emerge, indeed the very devil himself.

This you should note and understand when reading the above words and distinctions.

Chapter 39

If you ask: "What is a divinized or a sanctified[173] person?" my answer would be: The person who transmits and radiates the eternal and divine Light and burns with divine love, that person is sanctified or divinized.

We have already dealt with that Light somewhat. But let it be clear that the Light—or the inner recognition of the Light—is nothing, or is good for nothing, without love. This truth becomes plain from the following. A person may have an excellent knowledge of the difference between virtue and wickedness; yet, if he does not love virtue, he is not truly moral, for then, in effect, he obeys the unvirtuous and leaves virtue behind.

But if he loves virtue, he obeys it and his love renders the immoral[174] an enemy; he simply cannot indulge in it. He hates it in all humans. His love for virtue prompts him to practice and do the moral wherever he can. He does it without concern for reward or the why and wherefore of personal ends. He does it only because virtue is part of his love.

Virtue becomes for such a person its own reward. He is well content with this and does not accept treasures or riches in exchange. Such a person is or becomes truly moral.[175] A genuinely moral human would not accept the whole world if it might mean being immoral.[176] No, he would rather die a miserable death.

It is the same way with righteousness.[177] Many people know full well what right and wrong are, yet are not or will not become righteous thereby. When you do not love righteousness you actually practice wickedness and unrighteousness.[178] But if a person loves righteousness he would simply not wish to act unrighteously. Thus, if he is the enemy of unrighteousness, he becomes prepared to suffer and act vicariously wherever he detects unrighteousness in a fellow being, striving to remove the unjust condition and restore the wrongdoer to righteousness.

The truly righteous would rather die than cause unrighteousness and this for no other reason than for love of righteousness.

Righteousness becomes the reward of the truly righteous; she gives herself as reward. This is how a righteous person lives. He would rather die a hundredfold than live unrighteously. What we have said about righteousness or justice can also be said about truth.

Man knows a great deal about what is true, false, or

guileful. But if he does not love the truth, he is not truthful. On the other hand, if he does love the truth, the same happens to him as with respect to righteousness. Isaiah, in the sixth chapter, says about righteousness: Woe, woe unto all those who have a spirit of duplicity, that is those who appear good on the outside but inwardly are filled with lies and in their mouth lies are found.[179]

It is clear, then, that schooling and knowledge are worth nothing without love. One sees this with the devil. He is informed and knowledgeable about what is wicked and what is good, right and wrong, and the like. But since he lacks love for the Good, which he knows, he becomes averse to the Good. Yet the Good would prevail with him if he possessed love for the truth and for other virtues that he recognizes. No doubt that love must become part of rules and learned by knowledge, but if love does not accompany knowledge, nothing comes out of it.

It is also this way with God and things of God. A person may know much about God and God's qualities and therefore think he grasps and knows what God is. But if there is no love, that person will not become sanctified or divinized. However, if true love is to be united with knowledge, man must cling to God and let go of everything that is not God or is not of God. And whatever form the latter takes, he is its foe and adversary. It goes against his grain and is for him an affliction. This love unites man with God in such a manner that he nevermore will be separated from it.

Chapter 40

On the basis of what has been said so far we have to ask: How can the two following assertions exist side by side? For we have, first of all, said that knowledge about God without love for God never leads to blessedness. This sounds as if there would be a certain knowledge regarding God even though there is no love for Him.[180] Then, secondly, we have said earlier: Wherever God is truly known, He is also loved; in the very knowledge of God there is also love for Him.

How do these two statements agree? Note one thing here. We have talked about two lights, a true one and a false one. By the same token there are also two kinds of love, true and false. Each kind of love must be informed or guided by its own light or inner knowledge. Now, the true Light makes for true love, the false light makes for false love. For whatever the light in question considers the best and most desirable it brings home to love as the best and most desirable possession and enjoins love to love the content of its delivery. And love follows suit.

We said that the false light is of the natural order and nature itself. Its characteristics and marks are consequently everything in the natural world, namely I, Mine, Me, and so on. Therefore it must needs be inwardly deceived, and false. For no I and no Mine ever came to the true Light and to undefiled inner knowledge. Such wholeness is to be found only in the persons of the divine Trinity.[181] If one is to come to inner knowledge of the one truth, the I and the Mine must depart and get lost.

It is a mark of the natural, false light that it is avidly bent on as much learning as possible. It derives much pleasure, joy, and glory from its schooling and knowledge. It therefore asks for more and more learning and in this regard never comes to peace or fulfillment. The more and higher it probes in its quest for knowledge, the more it seems to enjoy and glory in the climb itself. When it comes so high that it thinks it knows all and is above all, it has arrived at its peak of enjoyment and glory. It comes to regard knowing as the best and the noblest. It instructs love to love the knowledge and learning it has garnered as the best and noblest there is. But knowledge and learning have in such a case become more loved than that which is the object of knowledge. Yes, the false natural light loves its knowledge and its learning more than that which should have been the object of knowledge. In fact the natural light is composed of knowledge and nothing else.

It is conceivable that this natural light could really know and grasp God and unadulterated, simple truth as it is in God were it not for one thing: It cannot become liberated from its nature, which is concern about itself and the things of the self.

In this sense we face here a mental and spiritual knowledge without love for that which is known. It rises and climbs so high that it finally develops the fanciful notion that it can actually know God and the unadulterated, simple Truth. But what it really loves is still itself.

It is true that God can be known by no one or nothing but God. When natural man fancies that he knows God, he is thereby saying he *is* God. In fact, he presents himself as God and wants to be so considered. He thinks he richly deserves all good things that come his way and he believes he has a right to everything. He is convinced that he has risen above all the things of the world, that he has conquered and so forth. He even looks on himself as having transcended Christ and the Christ life.

But he actually denigrates the Christ life in his imagined detachment. For in reality he has no desire to be Christ; he wants to be the eternal God. How come? Because Christ and His life are contrary and burdensome to all nature and natural man wants no part of it. Natural man desires to be God in eternity, not man. Or he may wish to be the postresurrection Christ, light, pleasurable, and pleasing to nature. This is the best condition, says natural man, because he thinks it is best for *him*.

The false light and the false, deluded love provide knowledge and a measure of learning. But no love emerges from within them. Knowledge and learning are indeed more loved than that which is the object of knowledge.

No doubt there is a knowledge that we can term "learned insight." But it is no real knowledge. That is to say, one fancies himself as knowing much by hearsay, reading, and proficiency in the Scriptures and then terms this "knowledge" and says: "I know this or that." When we ask: "From where have you learned it?" the answer is: "I have read it in the Scriptures." This is termed learning and knowledge. However, it is not true knowledge but a *belief.* Through this kind of learning and knowledge many things are perceived and known, but, alas, they are not grasped in love.

There is a kind of love that must be called utterly false, namely when one loves with an eye to reward. For instance, one holds righteousness dear, not for righteousness's sake but in order to acquire something thereby. And if someone loves another person because of that person's possessions, or if we love God for an ulterior purpose, for the sake of a certain thing we want to possess, that is all love gone astray. This love is actually steeped in the concerns of natural man. And nature as nature is capable of and knows no other love than that one. For to a discerning observer it is obvious that nature as nature loves nothing but itself. The Good is duly acknowledged but not an object of love.

But true Love is informed and guided by the true Light and knowledge. The true eternal divine Light inspires love to embrace nothing but the truly simple, perfect Good, for no other reason but goodness itself, and *not* in order to receive it as a reward or any one thing from God, but just out of love of goodness, because it is good and should therefore properly be loved.

Thus what is known about the true Light must also be loved in true Love. The perfect Good called God cannot make itself known except through the true Light. Therefore God must be loved when known.

Chapter 41

We add the following about true Light and true Love. When true Light and true Love are present in a person, the true perfect Good has come to be genuinely known and loved for its own sake. Not so that true Love and Light themselves are engaged in self-love, loving themselves for their own sakes. It is rather the case that this Love is directed to the true, simple Good. The Perfect can and will not love anything but the One, true Goodness— and this happens to the extent to which Love has been allowed to enter.

Since the Perfect is precisely this, it must love itself, yet not itself as a self and not for its own sake but in the sense that the one true Good loves the one, true, perfect Goodness and that true perfect Goodness is loved by the one, true, perfect Good. In this sense one says and rightfully so: "God does not love Himself as a self." For if there were something better than God, God would love that and not Himself.

In this true Light and in this true Love, I, Mine, Me, You, Yours have no abiding refuge. Rather, the true Light knows and proclaims that there is a Goodness that is *all* goodness—indeed above all goodness—and that all good things are united in one Being, in the One.

This Light likewise knows that without the One there is no good. That is why in this one Being love is not just an attachment to a particular thing, to an I, a You, or any separate thing, but to the One alone, in whom there is neither an I, nor a You, nor any other separate thing. It is in the One that all goodness is love as one Good.

This is according to the saying: "All in one as One and One in all as All." We love all good things by virtue of oneness in the One and for love of the One, out of the love we have for the One.

All concerns about the I, Mine, self, and things connected with them must be utterly lost and surrendered, except, of course, the traits that are necessary for our existence as persons. Thereby we tune into God whose innermost characteristic is such freedom.[182] What happens in a truly divinized person, be it in action or silent suffering compassion, happens in this Light and in this Love. Action and compassion stream out of them, manifest because of them, and flow back into them.

There is in this person an inner contentment and calm, untroubled by the urge to know more or less, to possess, to live, to die, to be or not to be, and similar strivings—they all become immaterial. That person does not complain about anything but the power of sin. What sin is, we have previously called the desire to seek something other than the simple, perfect Truth and the one eternal Will. To put it differently: to assert self-will in independence of and against the eternal Will.

The result of this—lying, fraud, unrighteousness, treachery, and other kinds of wickedness, sin for short— has only one explanation: We desire things contrary to God and the true Good. If only the one Will prevailed, there would be no sin. Hence it is proper to say that self-will is sin and this sums up what later emerges from it in various forms.

This is the only thing about which a truly divinized person complains. But his complaint and his lament are so strong, such a pain, that he or she would rather die a hundred times in shame and suffering than be led into the sins we have mentioned. This kind of sorrow in a world of sin must remain until the death of the body.

Where this inner sensitivity does not exist, we know for a fact that we are not dealing with a divinized person.

Now, from within this Light and this Love we love all

goodness as stemming from one source, as One, yes we love it as the One in all and everything. Therefore, all those things must be loved which man has come to know as truly good: virtue, order, rectitude, righteousness, truthfulness, and so on. All that which belongs to God and true Goodness, God's characteristics, is loved and praised through such signs. What is contrary to them and lacks them spells suffering and pain and is bewailed as sin; and, indeed, that is how sin arises.

The person in whom life is lived in true Light and in true Love leads the highest and noblest, best, and worthiest life that ever was and ever will be. Hence it must needs be loved and lauded above all other modes of life. In Christ this life was and is present in perfect form, else he would not be Christ. This love for the noble life and for all goodness makes it possible willingly and gladly to do and to suffer everything that must be done and suffered under God's providence, however heavy it may be for natural man to accept it.

Christ says about this: My yoke is sweet and my burden is light.[183] This experience stems from love for the noble and precious life. That becomes clear when we study the apostles and the martyrs. They suffered willingly and gladly the afflictions that befell them. They did not demand from God that he should shorten or lighten or diminish the tribulations. They asked only for steadfastness. In truth, everything pertaining to divine Love as it appears in a divinized person is really so very simple, plain, and forthright that it always eludes adequate descriptions in word or writing. All that the divinized can say is that he knows because it is. The person who does not have it cannot believe in it. How could he then have any knowledge of it?

There is that opposite, merely natural life, where a subtle, cunning, clever mind set prevails. It is so manifold and intricate and seeks and finds so many angles, so much falsity, so much treachery and self-love, that it is equally difficult to dress it in words or set it forth in writing.

All falsehood is rooted in illusion, all deception begins in self-deception. We can say this also about the false light and life. For, I repeat, he who deceives is deceived. In this false life and light and the love pertaining thereto we find all the things of the devil and his world. There is no difference between the two. For the false light is the same as the devil and the devil is this false light.

You will see it if I put it this way. The devil thinks he is God, or would like to be God or regarded as God Himself, and he lets himself be deluded into this kind of thinking. He is so deluded that he firmly believes he is not deluded. Well, that is precisely the way it is with the false light and its particular love and life. As the devil burns with desire to delude all humans, and to draw them to himself and mold them in his image, bringing much cunning and trickery to the task, exactly the same happens in the thralldom of this false light.

Just as there is no way to turn the devil from his designs, so it is here, in the light of illusion. It all comes from the fact that the two, devil and nature, imagine that they are *not* deluded; they believe they are doing famously. That is, of course, a most wicked and damaging fallacy. Thus the devil and nature are one. When nature is conquered the devil is conquered.[184] Obversely, when nature is not conquered, the devil is not conquered.

The false light abides in its delusion, whether it is directed toward the worldly or the spiritual realm. It is itself deluded and it insinuates its own delusion into people wherever it has a chance. From what has been said above it should be possible better to understand and know that we do not deal with a difference between the devil and nature.[185] Whenever we speak of the first Adam, disobedience, the old man, the I, self-will, self-serving, egoism, Mine, nature, false light, devil, sin, we speak of one and the same thing. And it is all contrary to God and exists without God.

Chapter 42

It may be asked: Is there anything that is contrary to God and the true Good? My answer is no. By this we have also said that there is nothing without God except one thing: to will otherwise than the eternal Will. The eternal Will desires that nothing but the true Good be loved. When things develop differently they are contrary to that eternal Will. In this sense it is true that he who is without God is working at cross-purposes with God. Yet in the very depth of it all nothing is contrary to God or contrary to the true Good.

One should understand it as though God would say: "He who wills without Me, who does not will as I will or differently from Me, wills contrary to Me.[186] My will is that no one should will otherwise than I, or without Me. No will should be without My will. Since being, life, or particular things do not exist without Me, no will should be without Me and My will."

As all beings are in truth one in the perfect Being and all good things are one good in the one Being and cannot exist without the One, all wills are meant to be one will in the one perfect Will and no will outside the one Will. The farther we are from this realization, the farther we are from the right path. We are engaged in unrighteousness and therefore in sin. We repeat: All willing apart from God's will is sin, that is to say, self-will, wrought up in the desires of one's own will.

Man will seek his own good, what he considers his own best, as though it were his possession and had to be

for his own personal sake and emanated from himself—
but in this way he will never find what is best for him.[187]
As long as man does his seeking in this manner, he is actually not on the way to that which is best for him. How,
then, could he find it? For as long as he persists in this
manner, he is out for himself and fancies himself to be the
best and highest. But since man is, in truth, not the best
and the highest, he does of course in fact not seek the best
and the highest while he is looking out for himself.

On the other hand, we find the highest and the best
in any person who seeks, loves, and intends the Good as
Good, for the sake of the Good, genuinely for the love of
the Good, not on behalf of the ego, the I, the Mine, the
Me, for personal gain, and from attitudes of this kind.
This is the right way to seek the highest and the best.
When done in other ways the search is false.

Verily, this is how the true and the perfect Goodness
channels its yearning, intention, and love through man,
and this is the way it finds itself. It is a great folly for
man, or any creature, to imagine that he knows or can do
anything by himself, especially to imagine that he knows
and can do anything good to earn ample merits and gain
much ground before God.[188]

If man rightly understood, he would see that he offers God a sham by such attempts. But God in His true
goodness is indulgent toward man, who in his vain and
awkward ways knows no better. God lets him prosper to
the extent of his ability to handle it and gives him as many
good things as he can receive. God is glad for man to have
the good things.

Yet I repeat that man can neither find nor receive
God while he lives in that condition. For unless the claims
of the I are abandoned, he will not find, nor receive.

Chapter 43

He who grasps and knows what the Christ life is also grasps and knows Christ himself. Conversely, he who does not know what this life is does not know Christ. He who believes in Christ also believes that the Christ life[189] is the noblest and best.

He who does not believe this does not believe in Christ. As much Christ life as there is in a person, that much of Christ there is also in him; and as little of the one, as little of the other.[190] For where the Christ life is, Christ is also present. Where this life is not, Christ is not.

In the Christ life one speaks with Saint Paul, who writes: I live, yet not I, but Christ lives in me.[191] This is life at its noblest and best. For where that life is, God Himself is and lives, with all goodness. How could there be a better life?

We speak of obedience, of a new man, of true Light, of true Love, and of the Christ life, yet it all means the same. Where one of these parts of true Life is, they all are. Where one of them breaks down or is absent, none of them can be present. For they are all of one piece in the realm of truth and being.

You should cling only to that by which you will obtain this life—and to nothing else—so that it may be born and come alive within you. Everything that leads away from it, abandon that, shun it. He who receives this life in the Holy Sacrament has received Christ truly and well. The more you receive of the life of the Sacrament the more you receive of Christ; the less you receive of it, the less you receive of Christ.

Chapter 44

You have heard it said that a person who has all his contentment in God has enough and to spare. This is true. Conversely, he who lets himself be satisfied with particular things in this world derives contentment from nothing pertaining to God. If you are content in God, you also find rest in nothing but the Oneness and the All, which is never this or that particularity.[192] For God is and must be One, He is All and must be All. What exists without being the One is not God. Likewise, what is and is not all and above all can never be God. For God is One and above all. He is All and above all.

He who has his contentment in God is satisfied with and in the One and only in the One as One. And unless a person can see all things as part of the One and one as all things and experience a something[193] and a nothing as the same, he cannot rest content in God.

But where a person does have such a vision, there comes this satisfaction—and in no other way. Moreover, he who surrenders wholly to God and becomes obedient to Him must have that serene resignation and obedience in compassionate sufferance, which means that he does not resist or defend or evade.

If you are not resigned and submissive to all around you within the One as the only One, you have really not surrendered to and begun to obey God.

We can study Christ in this regard. And he who wants to be still in God must have sufferance and be still in Him as the only One, and resist no suffering whatsoever. Christ did this.

He who resists the suffering involved and fends it off does not wish or is not able to suffer with God and be still in Him.[194]

Know this: No creature should be resisted with violence or with war, whether in intent or in deed. But we can, of course, prevent adversity and suffering, avoid it, flee from it—that is no sin. Now, if you wish to love God you shall love all things in one as the One, yet all, and you should love the One in all as all in One.

If we harbor love for something particular apart from the One and not for the sake of the One, we do not love God. For in that case we love things that are not God, we love them more than God. If we love something more than God or things divine, we do not really hold God dear. For God must and desires to be loved alone and, in truth, nothing should be loved but God alone. Where the true Light and the true Love are in a person, nothing but God is loved for there God is adored as Good and for the sake of the Good, all good things as One, One as all good things. Of a truth, all is One and One is all in God.

Chapter 45

Some might say: If one is to love all things, should he then also love sin? The answer is no. When we use the word *all* we mean the Good. All things that exist are good in the root of their existence.

The devil is good as part of existence. You cannot in that sense say that anything is evil or bad.[195] But sin is to intend or desire or love differently from God and that kind of willing is not part of being. Therefore it is not good. No particular thing is good except to the extent to which it is in God and lives with God.

Now, all things dwell as beings in God's being; their being is more truly in God than in themselves.[196] Hence we say that all things are good according to their innermost being. That in our lives which is not being-in-God should not be termed good.[197] Since God does not accept willing and intending that go against His will or are different in kind from Him, we can say about such things that they are evil, nongood, or even nothingness.

God loves deeds but not all deeds. Which ones then? Those that grow out of the teachings and instructions of the true Light and the true Love and the power that emanates from these and are done in truth and what pertains to truth—that belongs to God's innermost and it pleases Him greatly.

But deeds that come out of the false light and the false love are all wicked. This is especially true of that which is omitted, done, or suffered on the basis of another will or desire or another love than God's will and His love, that which occurs apart from God and contrary to Him. It is all contrary to God's work and the only word for it is sin.

Chapter 46

Christ said: He who does not believe or does not want or cannot believe, he is and will be condemned and lost.[198] This is indeed true. For a person who has come into the realm of time and who, of and by himself, has no knowledge cannot arrive at knowledge unless he first believe. If we strive to acquire knowledge about God before and apart from any belief at all there will be no entry for true knowledge.

I do not have in mind at this point the articles of Christian belief, for everyone accepts them. They are common assumptions among Christian folk, whether sinners or saints, wicked or good.[199] One must believe them, otherwise one cannot come to know them. I speak rather of something in truth itself that it is possible to know and experience but that truth must be believed before one may know and experience it. True knowledge will never come to you otherwise. Christ speaks of this belief in the saying I quoted.

135

Chapter 47

One says that self-will is the most widespread commodity in hell. That is certainly true. Hell is and consists of self-will. If there would be no self-will there would be no hell and no devil.[200] When we read that the devil, Lucifer, fell from heaven[201] and turned away from God, and so forth, it means only that he was anxious to maintain his own self-will and that he did not wish to tune his will to the eternal Will.

This was also the case with Adam in paradise. When we say self-will we mean willing to be other than the one eternal Will wills. But what is paradise? All things that *are*, for everything that *is*, is good and pleasing—yes, pleasing also to God. Therefore creation should be termed what it is, namely, a paradise.

It has been said that paradise is a *precinct* of the kingdom of heaven. By that token everything in our existence is truly a precinct of the Eternal or Eternity. This is especially true of the signs of God and Eternity that can be seen and known in our temporal life, among temporal things, in and with created beings. For the created world provides directions and paths to God and Eternity.

Thus this world is a precinct to Eternity. That is why we may safely call it a paradise.[202] In this paradise all things are lawful save one tree and the fruit thereof. This means: In all that exists around us nothing is forbidden, nothing is basically contrary to God, save one thing. That one thing is self-will, or to will and intend otherwise than the eternal Will wills.

Keep in mind that when God speaks to Adam He speaks to each human being: "What you do and what you leave undone, whatever comes to pass, it is all a welcome to you and permitted, as long as it does not take place for your own gain or in accordance with your own will, but flows out of and is in accordance with My will."[203]

But whatever happens guided by your will is contrary to the eternal Will. Not that every work wrought in this world would be against the eternal Will. But our works do become adversary deeds when they flow out of a will other than that of God, other than the eternal Will.

Chapter 48

You may ask: Seeing that this tree called self-will is so contrary to God and the eternal Will, why has God then created and instated it and placed it in paradise? I answer: Whoever among men and other beings demands to know the hidden counsel and Will of God, desiring to learn why God has done this or that or left this or that undone, that person insists on the same as Adam and the devil.

However long this hankering for disclosure endures, it will never be satisfied, which means, of course, that man is no different from Adam and the devil. For this urge to know God's plan rarely revolves around anything but the pleasure man takes in it and the glory he derives from it, and that is sheer pride.

A truly humble, illumined person does not demand that God disclose His secrets. He does not ask why God does or prevents this or that—and questions in a similar vein. He asks only how to become reduced and surrendering and how the eternal Will might become powerful in him, unhampered by other wills, and how the eternal Will may be fully manifested by and in him.

I can advance another answer on this matter. One may put it this way: The noblest and most delightful traits in created beings are knowledge or reason, on the one hand, and will, on the other. These two are intertwined. Where the one is, is also the other. Were it not for these two powers there would be no reasonable creatures, only brutes and brutishness.

It would be like a great emptiness, for God would

never receive of His own, there would not be any testing and realization in creation of His own characteristics. But such testing is necessary and part of the work toward perfection.

But now are knowledge and reason created and given together with will. Knowledge and reason are to instruct the will—and themselves—that neither knowing nor willing is on its own or that none of them is or should be a separate self; they should not promote or obey themselves in separation. Neither should they think of usefulness only in terms of what promotes their own separate achievements and ends, using themselves for themselves and for the sake of themselves.

No, reason and will proceed from the undivided One, they belong to Him, should submit to Him, return to Him, and become reduced to nothing in themselves, that is to say, in their self-dom.

Chapter 49

Let us consider, then, more especially, what the will is like. The eternal Will abiding from the beginning in God's Being, without activity and outward manifestation, is part of man, or in all beings, as working and willing power. For it is a sign and token of the will to extend itself in desire. Otherwise it would be in vain, empty, without deeds. Active willing cannot take place without creatures. Hence there must be creatures. God desires them so that the divine will may take shape through them, acquiring its own work. And I speak here of a will that is and must be without activity in God.

The will lodged in the creature, called the created will, is just as much God's will as what we term the eternal Will and it is not the property of the creature. So, as God cannot will by work and outward movement without creatures, he carries out deeds through them.

The creature should therefore not exert its will in separation but God alone should—and desires to—express His will in the creature by outward deeds. This will is thus in man, yet it is God's. Wherever in man or in other creatures this will would be purely and fully present, you would find a desire guided not by man but by God. There the will would not be self-will; nothing would be willed that could not be attuned to God's will. For God would do the willing there, not man, and the will would be one with and flow into the eternal Will.

But in this person are and remain pleasure and pain, joy and sorrow. For the human will attuned to God continues to experience both pleasure and pain. When things coincide with our will, we are comfortable and like it. When things go against the designs of our will, we experience pain. This pleasure and this pain are not called forth by man but by God. For the sources of pleasure and pain are the same as the will's.[204]

The will is not man's but God's. Both pleasure and pain are received from His hands. No lamentation is heard here against anything but that which is contrary to God. Conversely, no joy emerges there that is not a joy that grows out of God and all the signs of God.

As it is with the will, so it is with knowledge, reason, power, love, and everything that moves in man: It is all God's domain, not man's.

Where the will is entirely surrendered the rest would certainly be surrendered, too. This is how God would receive back His own and how, at the same time, man's will would not be his own. God has created the will but not in order that it become self-will.

Chapter 50

Now come the devil and Adam—that is to say, false nature—and take hold of this will and make it their own and use it to their own ends and for themselves. And this is the mischief, the unrighteousness, Adam's bite into the apple. It is forbidden since it is contrary to God. But as long as the enchantment lasts and self-will rules, there never is true peace. One sees that plainly both in people and with the devil: never any peace.

True blessedness can never reign where self-will rules, whether it be in our human time or in the age to come. I mean the bent toward claiming the will as one's own and for oneself.

If such a person's self-will is not surrendered in our human time but is carried out of time into the other realm, we may reasonably predict that there may never be contentment, peace, calm, or blessedness. This is obviously true of the devil.

If reason and will were not part of man, God would verily remain unknown, unloved, unpraised, unglorified, and no creatures would have any worth; they would be useless to God.

Thus I have answered the question of why God has created the will. It would be well pleasing to God if someone would be moved to repent as a result of my many words—which are, however, to the point and profitable, seen in the divine perspective.

What is free belongs to no one. If you usurp a free thing for yourself you commit a wrong. Among all free things nothing is more unbound than the will and should you usurp it and not leave it in its precious unboundedness, in its unfettered nobility, to its free ways, you commit a wrong.[205] The devil and Adam do this, as well as all their followers. But if you leave the will to its noble freedom, you do the right thing. Christ does this, as well as all His followers. If you deprive the noble will of its freedom, making it your own, sad requital will befall you; you will be burdened and possessed by sorrows, dissatisfaction, discontent, disquiet, vexation, yes, every kind of misfortune, and this condition will stay with you throughout time and into eternity.

Wherever there is a person in whom the will is not enslaved but remains noble and free, there we deal with a true, free, unfettered being of the kind about which Christ speaks: "The truth will make you free." And soon thereafter: "So if the Son makes you free, you will be free indeed."[206]

Chapter 51

I also draw to your attention that the proper use of your will is the use you make of it in the freedom we have described. There are no restrictions in a will thus molded. It chooses the noblest and the best in all circumstances. In such a state the will unerringly senses what is not noble and not good and this sensitivity causes it sorrow and grief.

Therefore, the freer and more unfettered the will grows, the more pained, grieving, and sorrow-filled it becomes, under the weight of surrounding ill will, wickedness, immoral practices, in short, by everything we term sin.

This becomes clear in Christ's life. He was the freest, most unfettered, least I-bound will that ever appeared, ever was, ever will be in human form. In His humanity He was thus the freest and the most unencumbered creature, yet in His humanity was also the most intense sorrow and grief and suffering over sin (which is all that wars against God) that can ever find room in a created being.

But when you usurp freedom for yourself in such a way that there is no room for grief and sorrowing over sin and what goes contrary to God; when your life turns heedless and careless; when you claim to be, in your present life, as Christ was after His Resurrection—then you have no true divine freedom, the one that springs from a true divine Light. Rather, here is a natural, unrighteous, false, deceptive, satanic freedom coming from a natural, false, deceptive light.

If self-will did not exist there would be no interest in doing only what one desires. In the kingdom of heaven there is no ownership and, as a result, instead there is contentment, true peace, and felicity.

Should someone in the kingdom of heaven claim something as his own, he would be prompted toward hell by his very claim, and he would turn into a devil.

In hell everyone wants to have a self-will. Therefore all is misery there, and wretchedness. The case is, correspondingly, the same in our temporal existence. Supposing a denizen of hell surrendered his self-will and were released from his desire to call something his own. He would then come out of hell into the kingdom of heaven.

In this earthly life man finds himself between heaven and hell. He can turn his will to whichever he chooses. The greater the desire to possess and own, the more hell and wretchedness he will have; the less self-will, the less hell and the closer to the kingdom of heaven.

The kingdom of heaven will assuredly be for the person who lives on this earth wholly without self-will and without the urge to possess for himself, informed by the true, divine Light, unencumbered, free, abiding in the ground of Being.

As soon as you hold onto something of your own, or desire to have it, you yourself become owned. But he who has nothing of his own, or does not desire to have and own, is unencumbered and free and slave to no one.

Chapter 52

All that has been written here Christ taught through-out His life of thirty-three and a half years, long in comparison with the brevity of these words: "Follow me." It is a brief word but if you are to follow Him you must surrender all things, just as everything was surrendered in Him, so completely that no other creature has done the like of it, or will ever do.

Furthermore, if you wish to follow Him you must take the cross upon you. The cross is the same as the Christ life and that is a bitter cross for natural man.[207] Christ says about the cross: He who does not leave all and does not take the cross upon himself is not worthy of Me and is not My disciple and follows Me not.[208]

But the falsely free natural man thinks that he has indeed left everything behind. The trouble is, however, that he does not *want* the cross and says that he has had enough of the cross and never needs it any more. That is self-deception.

If natural man had ever tasted the cross, he would, on the contrary, never leave it.

Anyone who believes in Christ must believe all that has been written here. Christ says: "No one comes to the Father but by Me."[209] We will note here how one shall come to the Father by way of Christ.

Man should guard his self and the things of the self inwardly and outwardly. That is to say, he should, as much as possible, conduct and preserve himself in such a manner that will, desire, love, or thought do not arise and live within him in ways other than those that are God's and would be fitting if God Himself were that man.

At points where one becomes aware that untoward things arise, things that are not of God, and are not fitting, one would strive to uproot them and withstand them at the first opportunity and as best as one can.

The same should apply to outward behavior, deeds or desisting from deeds, speaking up or keeping silent, waking or sleeping. Or let me say it this way: In his manner and deportment with respect to his own affairs and his relationship to others man should see to it that nothing happens but that which belongs to God's domain. Man must not turn to or permit anything to arise or remain within or outside himself that does not answer that test and he should ask the question: Would this act or omission be possible or fitting if God were to abide in man?

Whatever takes place in such a person's life, be it inward movement or outward, it would all be of God and that person would be a follower of Christ's life in human form, as we can understand and describe it.[210]

Chapter 53

If you lead a life such as the one just described, your going and coming would be through Christ. For you would be His follower. In this way you would also come with and through Christ to the Father. You would be a true servant of Christ. To serve Him is to follow Him, as He Himself says: "If anyone serves me, he must follow me,"[211] as though He would also say, obversely, "He who does not follow me does not serve me either."

He who follows Christ by serving Him thus arrives at the place where Christ dwells, that is, the Father. Christ tells us this when He says: Father, I will that where I am my servant should be there also.[212] Lo, the person who walks this way walks through the door into the sheepfold, that is to say, into the eternal Life, and the doorkeeper opens for him. He who chooses another way or imagines he can come to the Father or to eternal blessedness apart from Christ is deluded, for he does not go along the right path and not through the right door; so it is not opened for him. He is a thief and a murderer, as Christ says.[213]

Watch therefore whether or not you are living in undisciplined freedom and permissiveness and in neglect of boundaries[214] between virtue and vice, order and disorder, and the like. In other words, you must become aware whether or not you are treading the right path toward the right door. For neglect of the boundaries was not in Christ, nor is it in any of His true followers. Christ says: No one can come to Me unless the Father draws him.[215]

Note now that I understand the Father to be the perfect, the simple, total Good, which is all, above all, without which, outside of which, there is no true being and no true good and without which no true work was ever performed or ever occurs. And as the Good is all, it must also be in and for itself and above all.[216]

This exalted Goodness cannot be anything of that which a created being as created being may grasp and understand. For what created beings as such can grasp and understand follows the condition of creatureliness, which means particular things, this or that—and then we are back at the confined condition called creature.

If the Perfection that is Wholeness would be something particular or something that a created being grasps, it would not be the All, nor that which exists in and for itself; it would not be Wholeness. The perfect Wholeness therefore has no name;[217] it is none of that which the creature, guided by its creatureliness, can grasp or understand, recognize, think, or name. But when this perfect, nameless Power flows into a person ready for it, pregnant so to speak, then it brings forth its only-begotten Son in that person, gives itself through the Son. Hence we call the perfect Good, Father.

Chapter 54

Let us now see how the Father draws us to Christ. When something of the perfect Good dawns upon and is revealed to the soul of man, in a glance or in a rapture, as it were, a desire to approach and unite with the perfect Good is engendered in it. As this desire grows, more and more is revealed to the soul and the more that is revealed the more that soul yearns and is attracted.

In this way a person is drawn into and enchanted by the union with the eternal Good. The Father is the one who draws; man is being taught by the same One who seeks him so that he cannot come into the union except through the Christ life. And now man puts on that life of which we have already spoken.

Let us read two words by Christ. First, "No one comes to the Father but by Me,"[218] in other words, "through My life." Second, "No one comes to Me unless the Father draws him,"[219] that is to say, "he takes human life upon himself and follows Me." He is then touched and drawn by the Father, in other words, the single-minded and perfect Goodness.

Saint Paul has the following words about this: "When the perfect comes, the imperfect will pass away."[220] This means that people in whom the Perfect is recognized, felt, and tasted will, as far as that is possible in earthly life, think nothing of created things in comparison with this perfect Goodness. They are correct in that persuasion. For apart from the Perfect and without it there is no true good, nor true being. If, therefore, you have, know, and love the Perfect, you have and know every good thing. What more or what other things does this person want? What meaning do the parts have for him or her, when all the parts are united in one Being?

Chapter 55

What I have said just now deals with the outward life. It is a path, an access to a true inward life. The inward life begins as follows. When man tastes the perfect Being, as far as that is possible in an earthly life, all created things, yes, even his own self, become like nothing to him.

As man comes to know the true situation, namely that the Perfect alone is the All and above all, it follows of necessity that he must ascribe all good things to the same perfect Good alone, not to a created being: life, being, power, learning, knowledge, deeds and rest from deeds must be ascribed to the highest Good. From this follows also that if man does not claim anything for himself in a proprietary sense, neither life, nor being, neither power nor knowledge, neither deeds nor omission of deeds, indeed nothing one may generally call good, then he becomes poor and is reduced to nothing as a self; likewise reduced is the importance of every single item, which is to say all created things.

Then begins, first of all, a true inward life; from hence onward God himself becomes the person in such a fashion that there is nothing that is not God or things of God and also so that there is nothing left in man of which he considers himself to be proprietor.

Thus God is at work in man, living in him, knowing, empowering, loving, willing, doing, and resting. I am speaking of God as the One, Eternal, Perfect, that which exists in and for Itself. This is how in truth it should or could be and where it is otherwise man might indeed fare better and things could be more satisfactory for him.

A good means to enter into life-in-God is to make sure that the best becomes my dearest choice so that it is a joy to choose the best, abide by it, and become one with it.

I am thinking of my earthly fellow beings in the first place. What is best in these creatures? Here is the answer: The best is the eternal, perfect Good and its manifestations as they shine forth, work, are known and loved.

What is that which is God's and belongs to Him? I answer: All that we rightfully and truthfully can call good. When one holds to the best that one can discern in creatures, keeps to it, and does not turn back, one gradually arrives at something better, and even better until one can know and taste that the eternal Goodness is a perfect Good, without measure, without number, above all goods in created form.

Chapter 56

Now if that which is best should be what we hold dearest and if we are to follow its beckoning, the eternal, only Good alone must be cherished above all and we must hold to it and become attuned to it as much as possible. If you are to ascribe everything good to the eternal, only Good—as we rightfully and truthfully should—we must also rightfully and truthfully attribute to it the beginning, the progression, and the end of our course. By this affirmation we also acknowledge that man and all created beings are nothing in themselves. This is the plain truth; you may say or sing whatever you please. Only in this way can we come to a true inner life.

What will happen then? What will be revealed? What is the nature of that future life? No one can say or sing thereof. What that life is like in reality has never been spoken of, never been known or imagined in man's heart.[221]

My long discourse above contains this, in brief: Rightfully and truly, there should be nothing in man that claims anything as its own, nor should man will, desire, love, intend, anything but God and the Godhead alone, that is to say, the one eternal, perfect Goodness.

As soon as this proprietary urge emerges within man or when he wills, intends, or desires other than the eternal Good, he is overstretching himself and causing a breach.[222]

Let me add another short remark: If you can come to the point where you are to God what your hand is to you, be content.[223] It must rightfully be that way. Truly, every creature, man in particular, owes this to God, for he is subordinated to Him.[224]

Further, when man arrives where he thinks that *he* has accomplished something, it is time to watch out lest the devil sows ashes over it all by inducing nature to seek and take her ease, rest, peace, and her own welfare and fall into a foolish, undisciplined freedom and spiritual sloth that is foreign to and far from the true life in God.

This happens to the person who has not gone on nor desires to follow the right path, leading to the right door, that is to say, to Christ, as we have said before, and imagines that one can come to the highest Truth by another path, or thinks this goal has already been attained. Whether or not this person has in truth attained is tested by Christ, who says: He who wants to enter by other ways than Me will never come into My kingdom, nor attain the highest Truth, but he is a thief and a murderer.[225]

May we abandon our selfish ways and die away from our own will and live only to God and His will. May we be helped to this by Him who surrendered His will to His heavenly Father, and Who lives and rules with God, the Father, in union with the Holy Spirit, in perfect Trinity.[226]

> Printed in Wittenberg by
> Johan Grünenberg AD fifteen hundred
> and eighteen.

Notes

Introduction

1. See the book's own introduction preceding the table of contents: God "has spoken" it. *Theologia Germanica* will be abbreviated *Th. G.* in the footnotes of the present book.

2. Georg Baring, "Neues von der 'Theologia Deutsch' und ihrer weltweiten Bedeutung," *Archiv der Reformationsgeschichte* /ARG/ 48 (1957): 6–7. Cited hereafter as Baring, "Neues." Johann Agricola reports about the Small Theologia: "As far as I can recall a German book was found in Prussia, at a house of the Order. The title is, 'A spiritual booklet about the right distinction between the old and the new man, what the old and the new man is. . . .' We must draw the conclusion from this that he [Agricola] himself knows from conversations with Luther, with whom he spent 1515–1516 in Wittenberg, that the fragment had been found 'at a house of the Order' . . . Luther's contacts with Königsberg are well-known. . . . From there came the briefer manuscript, which Luther first learned about." In the present account a distinction will be made between the "Small Theologia" of 1516 and the "Large Theologia" of 1518. Since the anonymous author lived in Frankfurt (am Main) he is frequently referred to as the "Frankfurter."

3. Among church-historical works to which I am indebted for these glimpses of the outer world around *Theologia Germanica*'s inner world, the following are the most important: Hjalmar Holmquist, *Kyrkohistoria*, 3 vols. (Stockholm: P. A. Norstedt & Söner, 2d ed. 1928–1931) 2:261–316; *Kirke-leksikon for Norden*, ed. Fredrik Nielsen, 4 vols. (Aarhus: Albert Bayers Forlag, 1900–1929); Adolf Harnack, *History*

of Dogma, 7 vols., 3d ed. (Boston: Little, Brown & Co., 1899–1900), 6:84–149; August Neander, *General History of the Christian Religion and Church,* 5 vols. (Boston: Crocker & Brewster, 1859), 5:23–40.

4. To gain a picture of The Friends of God I have used the following works: *Kirke-leksikon for Norden;* Neander, *General History of the Christian Religion and Church,* 1:380–412. Adolph Harnack, *History of Dogma,* 6:97–117; E. Filthaut, ed., *Johannes Tauler, Ein deutscher Mystiker* (Essen: Driever Verlag, 1961), pp. 37–74, 422–434; James M. Clark, *The Great German Mystics* (Oxford: Basil Blackwell, 1949), pp. 75–97.

5. Georg Baring, *Bibliographie der Ausgaben der "Theologia Deutsch," 1516–1961, Ein Beitrag zur Lutherbiographie* (Baden-Baden: Verlag Heitz, 1963), pp. 7–8. Hereafter cited as Baring, *Bibliographie....* On the Würzburg edition of *Th. G.* see the bibliographical notes later in the present Introduction. The Bernhart rendering referred to here is Joseph Bernhart, trans. and ed., *Der Frankfurter, eine deutsche Theologie* (Leipzig: Im Insel-Verlag, 1920). Hereafter cited as Würzburg-Bernhart.

6. Joseph Bernhart surmises that Luther, before turning over the anonymous manuscript of *Th. G.* to the printer, subjected it to a more logical organization, conceptually elucidated it, perhaps not without infusion of personal beliefs, and by and large acted as a critical redactor (Würzburg-Bernhart, pp. 208–209). The validity of this argument will be discussed in the bibliographical annotations of the present Introduction. (see pp. 49–52 and fn. 43.)

7. Material for the subsequent observations has been gleaned from various articles in *Kirke-leksikon for Norden* (see fns. 3 and 4); E. Filthaut, ed., *Johannes Tauler ...* ; Franz Pfeiffer, ed., *Deutsche Mystiker des vierzehnten Jahrhunderts* (Leipzig, 1857, new print Scientia Verlag Aalen, 1962); Susanna Winkworth, trans., *The History and Life of the Reverend Doctor John Tauler of Strasbourg* (New York: Wiley & Halsted, 1858); Hermann Büttner, trans. and ed., *Meister Eckeharts Schriften und Predigten,* 2 vols. (Jena: Eugen Diederich, 1921); Raymond Bernard Blakney, trans., *Meister Eckhart, A Modern Translation* (New York: Harper & Brothers, 1941); James Clark and John V. Skinner, trans. and eds., *Meister Eckhart, Selected Treatises and Sermons* (London: Faber & Faber, 1958).

8. In the work by A. Harnack already quoted in fn. 3, we read: "Mysticism is always the same; above all there are no ... confessional distinctions in it" (6:97). However, see Bengt Hägglund, *The Background of Luther's Doctrine of Justification in Late Medieval Theology* (Philadelphia: Fortress, 1971); Heiko Oberman, "Simul gemitus et raptus: Luther und die Mystik," in Ivar Asheim, ed., *The Church, Mys-*

ticism, Sanctification and the Natural in Luther's Thought (Philadelphia: Fortress, 1967); Bengt R. Hoffman, *Luther and the Mystics* (Minneapolis: Augsburg, 1976), esp. pp. 119–122. The latter work hereafter cited as Hoffman, *Luther*. . . .

9. Franz Pfeiffer, ed., *Deutsche Mystiker*, 2 vols. (Stuttgart: Scientia Verlag Aalen, 1962; reprint of ed. Leipzig 1857), 2. Meister Eckhart, Sermon 6, p. 33. Hereafter cited as Pfeiffer.

10. Susanna Winkworth, trans., *The History and Life of the Reverend Doctor John Tauler of Strasbourg*, sermon 19, p. 377.

11. Hoffman, *Luther* . . . , pp. 142–143.

12. Pfeiffer, 2:sermon 84, p. 269. Cf. C. de B. Evans, trans., *Meister Eckhart by Franz Pfeiffer* (New York: Lucis Publishing Co., n.d.), p. 211. Cf. also Würzburg-Bernhart, p. 78.

13. E. Filthaut, ed., *Johannes Tauler* . . . , p. 170.

14. Hoffman, *Luther* . . . , pp. 108–111.

15. I have found helpful imaginative suggestions about Tauler's world of thought in Rudolf Steiner, *Mysticism at the Dawn of the Modern Age*, trans. Karl E. Zimmer (Englewood, N.J.: Rudolf Steiner Publications, 1960), pp. 141–154.

16. Shorthand expressions like these cannot possibly do full justice to two hundred years of intricate academic discussion about the nature of Eckhart's theology. It is clear that the teaching about "God in man" always lives on the brink of pantheism, the doctrine that the universe as a whole is God. Eckhart was not a pantheist in that extreme sense. He made a distinction between "Godhead" and "God," that is to say the universe certainly does not exhaust the meaning and content of the divine. For accounts of debates on Eckhart's theology, see Blakney, pp. xiii–xxviii (present Intro. fn. 7) and Clark and Skinner, pp. 25–35 (present Intro. fn. 7).

17. Pfeiffer, *Meister Eckhart* . . . , p. 125 (present Intro. fn. 7).

18. Georg Hofmann, ed., *Johann Taulers Predigten* (Freiburg: Herder, 1961), pp. 405, 321.

19. Nathan Söderblom, *Till mystikens belysning*, ed. Hans Åkerberg (Lund: Studentlitteratur, 1975), pp. 12–28, 91–97.

20. Concerning the rather common supposition that Luther embraced mystical ideas in his youth, only to abandon all of them for a supposedly more evangelical reliance on outer signs and justification as "imputation" in his mature years, see Hoffman, *Luther* . . . , pp. 111–119, the section on "Mysticism differentiated."

21. The problem of self-will in a universe where everything occurs within God's purview is touched on in Chapter 47 of *Th. G.*

22. The following glimpses of the life and thought of the Broth-

ers and Sisters have been obtained from Neander, 5:392–407 (present Intro. fn. 3); Albrecht Ritschl, *Geschichte des Pietismus in der reformierten Kirche*, 3 vols. (Bonn: Adolph Marcus, 1880–1886), vol. 1; Würzburg-Bernhart, pp. 50–55; Hermann Mandel, ed., *Theologia Deutsch*, vol. 7, in the series *Quellenschriften zur Geschichte des Protestantismus*, eds. Joh. Kunze and C. Stange (Leipzig: A. Deichert'sche Verlagsbuchh. Nachf. Georg Boehme, 1980), pp. xliii-xlvi. Hereafter cited as Mandel.

23. Cf. *Th. G.*, ch. 27.

24. This posture is described in *Th. G.*, ch. 23.

25. The basis for the following remarks is Mandel, pp. xxii-xxxvi, as far as I know the only comprehensive account of the fortunes of the *Th. G.* throughout the centuries. Important information has also been gleaned from Baring, *Bibliographie* . . . which lists all known editions of *Th. G.* from 1516 to 1961. All prints of *Th. G.* published up to Luther's death in 1546 are treated in Joseph Benzing, *Lutherbibliographie* (Baden-Baden: Verlag Librarie Heitz, 1966) (hereafter cited as Benzing). With respect to individual leaders, basic information has been obtained from *Kirke-leksikon for Norden*.

26. Hunnius refers to ch. 14 in *Th. G.*

27. Baring, *Bibliographie* . . ., pp. 126–152.

28. Bengt R. Hoffman, "On the Relationship between Mystical Faith and Moral Life in Luther's Thought," *Bulletin, Lutheran Theological Seminary*, 55, no. 1 (February 1975): 21–35. Source references: *D. Martin Luther's Werke*, Weimarausgabe, 58 vols. (Weimar: Böhlaus, 1883–), 45; 532, 535, 536, 497–499 (hereafter cited as *W*); *Luther's Works*, H. T. Lehmann and J. Pelikan, eds. (St. Louis and Philadelphia: Fortress and Concordia, 1955–), 24; 78–83, 41–42.

29. Baring, "Neues," *ARG*, 1957, pp. 1–10; Baring, *Bibliographie* . . ., pp. 7–8, Mandel, pp. i–ii.

30. *W* 1; 153. The letter section of the same work, Briefwechsel, will be cited as *WB* and the Table Talk section, Tischreden, as *WT*.

31. *WB* 1; 79, 58–63. Luther to Spalatin: "If you want to read pure, solid theology, most akin to teachings of old, propounded in the German tongue, you should get hold of Johannes Tauler's sermons. I herewith send you, as it were, an abridgement of his entire art of proclamation. For I have not seen, in Latin or in our own tongue, a theology which is more wholesome and more in keeping with the Gospel" ("Neque enim ego vel in latina vel in nostra lingua theologiam vidi salubriorem et cum Euangelio consonantiorem").

32. *W* 1: 152–153. Facsimile of the entire *Eyn geystlich edles Buch-*

lcynn of 1516 in Baring, *Bibliographie* . . . , pp. 11–25, with the above
"Vor Rede" on p. 12. Further bibliographical information in Benzing, p. 14. Luther's reference to Dr. Tauler as a man of the Preaching
Order refers to the Dominican monastic community. The Reformer
found out later that Tauler could not have been the author, at any
rate.

33. Mandel, p. i, fn. 2.

34. Baring, *Bibliographie* . . . , p. 27. Luther's three marginal no-
tations in Latin can be found ibid., pp. 16, 17, and 23. They were
hardly meant for the printed stage, says Baring, ibid., p. 7, fn. 4,
against Mandel, p. ii. They were present in print I and print II of the
Small Theologia (Wittenberg, 1516, and Leipzig, 1518) but are not to
be found in the Large Theologia. On prints I and II see Baring, ibid.,
pp. 27–28. Since Luther's marginal remarks are supportive rather
than adversary we shall not devote space to them here.

35. Benzing, pp. 28–32. Mandel, pp. 4–114, presents the 1518
Wittenberg edition in a version that seems to harmonize between the
two prints. Mandel offers the differences as against the Small Theologia and the Würzburg edition of the Large Theologia, 1497. See Baring, "Neues," pp. 3ff. On Mandel's work, see Baring, *Bibliographie* ,
p. 138. Baring considers this "the complete" Luther edition but notes
that paragraphs and orthography are "arbitrary." On the Würzburg
edition, see fn. 42.

36. Baring, *Bibliographie* . . . , p. 30.

37. Baring, *Bibliographie* . . . , pp. 30, 32. The Würzburg edition
of 1497, which attaches content descriptions to each separate chapter
number, has obviously over a long period been considered to be closer to the original work, as can be seen from the frequency with which
it has been consulted by translators. However, it can be safely assumed that the way in which the present book is arranged is the way
in which Martin Luther found it and forwarded it to the typesetter at
the Gruenenberg printing shop.

38. Mandel, p. v.

39. Benzing, pp. 24–26.

40. Baring, *Bibliographie* . . . , p. 152.

41. Ibid., p. 60.

42. Ibid., pp. 125, 126. Since a number of references will be
made to the Würzburg text in the course of the present translation,
the following information about texts is now given: Pfeiffer, see fn. 9
of the present Intro. Another influential text is the reproduction of
the 1497 manuscript published by Willo Uhl, *Der Franckforter ("Eyn*

deutsch Theologia") (Bonn: Marcus & Weber, 1912). See Baring, *Biblio-graphie . . .* , p. 140. Two important renderings in modern languages have emanated from these basic works. First, Susanna Winkworth, trans., *Theologia Germanica:* Which setteth forth many fair Lineaments of divine Truth, and faith very lofty and lovely things touching a perfect Life. Edited by Dr. Pfeiffer from the only complete manuscript yet known (London: Macmillan & Co., 1874). Winkworth's translation, based on Franz Pfeiffer's edition of Würzburg 1497, has seen at least 14 editions and reprints (Baring, *Bibliographie . . .* , pp. 126, 128, 131, 132, 134, 135, 136, 140, 141, 142, 144; in 1949 W.'s trans. was radically changed to accord with Joseph Bernhart's German version; Baring, *Bibliographie . . .* , pp. 148, 150). This book in its 1874 form, will be cited hereafter as Winkworth. Second, Joseph Bernhart, trans. and ed., *Der Frankfurter . . .* , see fn. 5 of the present Intro. Bernhart based his version on Willo Uhl's reproduction of Würzburg 1497. Further eds. in German: 2d ed., 1922; 3d ed., 1946; trans. into English: eds. of 1949, 1950, and 1951. See notes concerning Winkworth's trans. Baring, *Bibliographie . . .* , pp. 140, 141, 146, 148, 150. Another early English trans.: Mrs. Malcolm, *Old German Theology.* A Hundred Years Before the Reformation. With a Preface by Martin Luther (London: Arthur Hall, Virtue & Co., 1854). See Baring, *Bibliographie,* p. 125. The Malcolm trans. is based on Biesenthal's German ed. of Leipzig 1518 (Luther's version). See Baring *Bibliographie . . .* , p. 124. A later English trans. is Thomas S. Kepler, *Theologia Germanica, The Way to a Sinless Life* (Cleveland & New York: World Publishing Co., 1952, 1961?). See Baring, *Bibliographie . . .* , pp. 150, 152.

43. Würzburg-Bernhart, p. 209. See reference to the same notation in fn. 6 of the present Intro.

44. Ibid., p. 208. Winkworth, the most widely read conveyor of *Th. G.* in English, thus assumes that Würzburg is the preferable text (p. xliv).

45. Mandel, p. ix.

46. *W*, 1; 376.

47. Baring, *Bibliographie . . .* , p. 8. Baring has in mind Dr. Max Pahnke's planned edition of a manuscript found in the State Library at Dessau.

48. Mandel, pp. ix–x. Mandel makes reference to Hermann Büttner, *Das Büchlein vom vollkommenen Leben.* Eine deutsche Theologie, in der ursprünglichen Gestalt herausgegeben und übertragen von Hermann Büttner (Jena: 1907). For details on Büttner's work, see Baring, *Bibliographie . . .* , pp. 135–136. Büttner, comments Mandel, "es-

says the impossible: to recover the original text of the *Theologia Germanica.*" Büttner should be given credit for according preference to the Luther text. But his edition deals with this persuasion without consistency. B. "adds in unnoticed ways the younger source" [Würzburg]. Mandel concludes with a statement that will remain valid as long as and until an original manuscript of *Th. G.* available to Luther is found: "We do not possess the means to restore the original form. Consequently, an attempt in that direction will needs be arbitrary. With Büttner we still do not have Luther's more original text before us since B. actually does not offer it directly."

49. Mandel, p. vii.
50. Baring, *Bibliographie . . .* , p. 125.
51. Mandel, p. viii.
52. Würzburg-Bernhart, p. 209.
53. Baring, "Neues," p. 3.
54. Baring, *Bibliographie . . .* , p. 138; Baring, "Neues," p. 3.

Theologia Germanica

Preface

1. Reference presumably to 2 Cor. 10:10. Several of the subsequent allusions to biblical passages are approximations or paraphrases. Luther often quoted from memory and occasionally bent the original a little to suit the point he wanted to make.

2. Reference presumably to 1 Cor. 1:17.

3. Reference presumably to Col. 2:3–4.

4. Reference presumably to Ps. 8:2.

5. Luther may refer to Prov. 10:20: "The tongue of the righteous is choice silver"; or to Is. 35:6: "The tongue of the dumb shall sing for joy."

6. Luther's term is *eynfeltig,* which literally means "made in one fold," "simpleminded." He may have had Prov. 3:34 in mind, where the word is "lowly." At any rate, Luther does not speak of feeble-minded humans but of persons who do not rely on glittering talents—they may in fact possess none—and make no claims for themselves.

7. Luther obviously refers to Ps. 14:6, which begins with the two Latin words cited. In translation they mean "the counsel of the powerless" (or "poor"). Luther paraphrases the verse. The Revised

Standard Version (hereafter cited as *RSV*) renders the passage as follows: "You would confound the plans of the poor, but the Lord is his refuge."

8. Luther here alludes to the mystical movement called "Germanic mysticism." It was part of the Gothic rebellion against Romanic stylization. It expressed the metaphysical longing of the soul. When Luther here concedes that he does not mind being referred to as a "German theologian" he actually professes adherence to a mystical theology that reckons with *experience* of God's indwelling and presence. He does not intend to be apologetic about it. As I have suggested in my book *Luther* ... (see Intro., fn. 8), Luther was pervasively aware of the inner, mystical side of justification by faith. In other words, what he felt about the presence of the "mystical Christ" in the year of this preamble to *Th. G.* was also what he felt in later years.

9. Again, the evangelical theology brought forth by Luther is considered to be "old" theology in the sense that it deals with enduring motifs of salvation and God-experience. The new German theologians in Wittenberg had brought to light old, essential knowledge of the God-man relationship. The Reformer finds that precisely the mystical tract *Theologia Germanica,* expresses the experience of God-in-Christ as Justifier. Because German Wittenberg theology integrates such experience with its reflection it is "the best."

10. Concerning the "Friends of God," see the introductory comments to the present English edition. This terse piece of information about the anonymous author likewise stems from an anonymous source. Luther may have written it, some scholars have suggested. But more likely it is that he found it in the copy, which he must have come across in 1518 and decided to print in its entirety.

11. The first index rubric alludes to 1 Cor. 13:10.

12. The adjective is *volkumen.* The noun employed at other points is *volkumenheit* (for instance Chap. 1 heading). I have chosen to translate these words as "perfect" and "perfection" in most instances, although I am aware of the moralistic ring they have acquired. *Th. G.* uses them more in the sense of "whole" and "wholeness," but these terms may, on the other hand, be too colored by nonreligious psychology to convey the meaning. However, at a few junctions where the context seems particularly fitting, they will be used here. *Th. G.* means by *volkumenheit* man's perfect integration with God, implying a growing consonance between body, mind, and spirit in earthly existence and a full union in the afterlife, where God becomes all in all.

13. See Hoffman, *Luther . . .* , pp. 164–165, and fns. 63, 64, 65 and

66. *Vergotten* is the Frankfurter's term. This could also be translated "sanctified" or "Godlike." Luther spoke of "conformation" to Christ as a process. Faith creates "divinity" in us, he says. Lutheran orthodoxy's and Lutheran historical-critical theology's distinction between "theological faith" and "actual change" (in man's psyche) moves us away from Luther. *Vergotten* can also be translated "be made a partaker in the divine nature."

14. The original used for this translation carries the words *hilfft ym zu dem aller pesten*. No doubt this is a slip of the index writer—or it may be a lax way of spelling *poesten*, i.e., "the worst," "the most evil." In the text proper we find these words: *hilfft ym zu dem aller poesten*, that is to say: "prompts him to the worst," to the most evil. A copy of the original edition, described in the Introduction, is in the present translator's and commentator's possession. It is called *Eyn deutsch Theologia, das ist Eyn edles Buchleyn* . . . , printed in Wittenberg by Johann Grünenberg, 1518. The discrepancy referred to above can be seen if one compares the title for Chapter 32 in the Index (A:3) with the text (F:3, line 4). In the latter the word is spelled *poesten*, "worst." H. Mandel has edited an almost identical version of Luther's first published work. He describes two 1518 Wittenberg printings of the book, an exemplar of the second being in my possession. The fn. references will be to Mandel's book, *Theologia Deutsch*, cited as Mandel. (See Intro. fn. 22.) The pp. regarding "pest" and "poest" in Mandel are 5 and 63. *Theologia Deutsch* will, as indicated, be cited as *Th. G.*, an abbreviation of the book's Latin title, *Theologia Germanica*.

15. The expression *ware gruntlich wesenliche demuttigkeit* refers to a humility that has been experienced in the very depth of man's being, and is "true" because it involves man's radical reduction before the face of God. Other kinds of humility are in the nature of play-acting.

Chapter 1

16. The corresponding Bible passage is obviously Saint Paul's dictum in 1 Cor. 13:10: "But when the perfect comes, the imperfect will pass away" (*RSV*). "The divided" can also be translated "that which is in part." I would like to draw attention to the previous use of "whole" and "wholeness" as English equivalents of *volkumen* (or *volkomen* as the Frankfurter has it in this particular place) and *volkumenheit*. In the present translation the context has determined whether "perfection" or "wholeness" should be used. But the reader should understand that the Frankfurter is very much concerned with *integra-*

tion of body, soul, and spirit, or *union* with God, whenever he uses the word *volkumen*. This is evidenced here by his rephrasing of Paul's "to be in part" into "divided," an unreal sense of dividedness, whose opposite pole is wholeness.

When Luther's edition of *Th. G.* speaks of God's "Being" it uses the term *wesen*. The personal pronouns for *wesen* are "he" and "it" used interchangeably. I have translated the alternatives as they appear in the text. The lack of consistency seems to me to illustrate the natural lack of adequacy one experiences when discussing the ultimate. The Würzburg edition of *Th. G.* makes it easier for itself by speaking of the ultimate as a *Wesenheit*, which is equipped with a *Wesen* and produces *Wesenheiten*, an "entity" with an "essence" issuing in "entities." With respect to the Würzburg edition of *Th. G.*, see the Introduction of the present book. It is, as noted, cited as Würzburg-Bernhart; page references are to the following work: *Der Frankfurter, Eine deutsche Theologie*, trans. and ed. Joseph Bernhart (Leipzig: Im Insel-Verlag, 1920). The latter is in modern German but maintains the original syntax.

17. The reference here appears to be Saint Paul's allusion to Greek thought in Acts 17:28: "In him we live and move and have our being." *Th. G.*'s use of "being," *wesen*, is not precise but the burden of the Frankfurter's proclamation is that God's *wesen* is the source, ground, and sustaining power in and around all separate beings; in fact, that God's being renders human feelings of separateness illusory. See further fn. 21 on "accidental" at the end of the present chapter. "Essence" or "being" (*wesen*) in the Frankfurter's account is not God as an entity but as an all-embracing *dynamis*.

18. Luther's edition has the following expression: "Darum nennet man das volkommen nit wan es ist dieser keins." Mandel edited and critically analyzed Luther's 1518 edition of *Th. G.* (see fn. 22 in the Introduction of the present book). He retouched the text in minor ways to render it more readable (see his fn. on p. x). In the dictum given above Mandel equipped the *nit* with quotation marks, not present in the Wittenberg edition, and made the word into a noun. The result is the following, in translation: "Therefore we term the perfect 'Nought' for it is none of its parts" (Mandel, p. 8). It should be noted that the Luther edition of *Th. G.* uses *nichtz* as noun and *nit* as adverb. But the meaning of the sentence remains the same in either case: The negative theology, *Theologia negativa*, expresses the otherness of God by referring to Him as the "Nought."

19. Würzburg (see fn. 16) has the following addition at this

point: "Its not-coming is wholly dependent on us and not on perfect Being. Similarly the sun sheds light on the whole world and is as near to one creature as to another, but a blind person cannot see it. The deficiency lies in the blind man, not in the sun. As the sun cannot hide its brightness but must shed light on the earth, so also God, the highest good, does not will to hide himself from anyone, wherever he finds a worshipping soul, radically cleansed from all creatures. For according to the measure of our putting off the creatures we are able to receive the Creator—neither more nor less. For if my eye is to see anything it must be purified from all other things. Where heat and light enter, cold and darkness must depart; it cannot be otherwise" (Würzburg-Bernhart, p. 94). Mandel comments: "The originality of the text Luther used is evident on account of the fact that [Würzburg] anticipates the answer" (Mandel, p. 9).

20. The text that Martin Luther had in front of him and that he published in Wittenberg in 1518 contains the term *meinheit* for the last posture in the enumeration. Würzburg's word in the same slot is *liebheytt*. It is rendered *Begehrlichkeit* by Joseph Bernhart, who considered the text he chose for his rendition (the Würzburg edition of 1497) as superior to Luther's choice (see Würzburg-Bernhart, p. 95 and fn. 8). The meaning of the words is contained in the Latin *concupiscentia*. Luther's edition expresses this better than Würzburg. *Meinheit* connotes a linkage between "me," "mine," and biophysical impulse, captivity in the body.

21. The Aristotelian meaning of the "accidental" nature of the created world is that it is not contingent on "substance." That which exists substantially does so in independence of the accidental. The author of *Th. G.* rather reflects the Neoplatonic view according to which there is an affinity and an interaction between the ultimate and the perfect, on the one hand, and the determinate world, on the other. The latter is conditioned by its eternal source and contingent upon it. Luther really never found this universal religious theme irreconcilable with his experience of the Gospel; this becomes especially clear if sufficient attention is paid to his description of faith as *sapientia experimentalis*, the felt presence of God. (See the discussion on *sapientia experimentalis* under "experience" in Hoffman, *Luther . . .*). It would thus be an error to ascribe the Aristotelian "substance-accidence" thinking to *Th. G.* The Frankfurter simply says that man's being is *in* that Being which alone can properly be said to have life. The Frankfurter's term *zufall*, accidence in the sense of nonessentialness, wants to convey that created beings have no being outside the ulti-

mate Being. One is reminded of Saint Paul's approving quotation from Greek wisdom: "In him we live and move and have our being" (Acts 17:28).

Chapter 2

22. There is an almost exclusively ethical ring to the Frankfurter's treatment of man's sinfulness. Mandel, p. 10, also draws attention to this fact and says that Augustine and Aquinas relate sin consciousness even to cosmic and psychological dimensions. The Frankfurter's notion of sin, however, is linked to one thing: that God wants to be the subject of the human will but finds that the human will wants to be its own subject. "The gauge is neither in the relation to two worlds nor in psychology but in the relation between two wills."

23. Würzburg here has the expression, ". . . und ein Eigen haben wollte." The edition used by Luther presents this version: ". . . uñ ym gehoret auch etwas tzu," (". . . something was his own property"). The latter brings out the devil's claim more graphically. Mandel suggests that concupiscence is the sin referred to here. That is to say, Adam's and the devil's sin is pride, a mental-spiritual waywardness. But when it turns up in the human orbit it becomes libidinous sin, carnal aberration (Mandel, p. 10, fn. 4). Mandel then confuses the issue somewhat by introducing this kind of carnal-material concupiscence in terms of "the cosmological ethic." In his comment at the beginning of this Chapter, Mandel after all *rejects* the idea that *Th. G.* puts a "cosmic" construction on the life in God (Mandel, p. 10, fn. 2).

Chapter 3

24. The words related to man are *mocht nit*—man is "unable"; the words related to God are *solt nit;* this expresses a "should" or "would," which is part of God's design. The Frankfurter's noun for restitution is *pessering* (verb: *pessern*). It is here rendered interchangeably as "amends," "redemption," or "healing" (verbs: amend, redeem, or heal).

25. Cf. Angelus Silesius's utterance that Christ might be born a thousand times in Bethlehem, yet were he not allowed to be born in the soul, that soul would be eternally lost. The remark is quoted by K. Barth in *Church Dogmatics* (Edinburgh: T. & T. Clark, 1960–   ), IV, 4:15. Barth disapproves of the notion. Mandel opines that we here, in *Th. G.*, see "the strange, unsatisfactory Germanic salvation teaching: man must become like Christ; Christ's only significance is to be a model for salvation. . . . The ideal is proclaimed for immediate imita-

tion. Sin ... and ... forgiveness" are "not recognized." Such critique of the Frankfurter is, it would seem, obverted by himself in, for instance, Chapters 13, 18, 23, 33, and 34. What he says about Christ's growing dominion can be compared with Luther's suggestion that we are called to become "little Christs" and that the soul may become "formed" in Christ (See Hoffman, *Luther* ..., pp. 176–177).

26. To surrender to God, to let God do what He alone can do, to "suffer" Him to do all the work in us—this was Martin Luther's constant reminder about the nature of justification. Mandel (p. 12, fn. 1, and p. xxxvi) suggests that Luther in this respect broke with Augustine, who tended to think dualistically about God. In the Augustinian view God was not present and at work in our world but rather was an entity beyond this world, of a substance wholly different from this world. Mandel considers this Platonic dualism. Thomas Aquinas, Mandel continues, changed that way of looking at the God-man relationship. From man's own knowledge of the world, said Aquinas, it must be obvious that God is the first cause. Thus the world and man are basically linked to each other. But also here there is in fact separateness between God and world. Instead of belief in creation we get deism. Luther was no less opposed to this mode of thinking Mandel maintains that "the Catholic idea of piety" emanated from Augustinian and Thomistic suppositions that placed God outside this world and made Him an object to which man had to relate himself as he relates himself to other objects. The reader may not agree with Mandel's generalizations. What is important in this context, however, is to see that *Th. G.* and Luther think in similar fashion about God's presence, breaking with the tradition of human exertion, spirituality as task rather than grace. God is present in man and he works in man's life. When Luther says that man ought to step aside and let God do his work, he expresses the same experience as the Frankfurter does here (see Luther quotes on this score in Hoffman, *Luther* ..., pp. 187–188).

Chapter 4

27. Is. 42:8 and 48:11.

Chapter 5

28. The Frankfurther here describes "quietism," the spiritual endeavor to render the soul so free from attachment that it is no longer involved in activity of any kind. It is possible, says Mandel (p. 13, fn. 2) that the teaching of Meister Eckhart is the target at this point. If

that is so, the Frankfurther would detach himself from Eckhart on this score, that is to say, if Eckhart's words about the stilling of all the movements of the soul and an immersion in the ground of the soul really mean something purely negative, then the Frankfurter would be against this notion. There must after all, he argues, be some concreteness to the idea of "God-in-man."

29. Würzburg adds a fairly long elaboration about how will, love, and good works do not emanate from man and illustrates this with three Bible passages: "Apart from me you can do nothing" (Jn. 15:5); "What have you that you did not receive?" (1 Cor. 4:7); "Not that we are sufficient of ourselves to claim anything as coming from us; our sufficiency comes from God" (2 Cor. 3:5).

30. Our present version of *Th. G.* edited by Luther has the word *geliebt*, "loved," instead of *ungeliebt*, "unloved." Würzburg has the logically correct *ungeliebt*. There is no saying whether the error existed in Luther's basic document or emerged only in Grünenberg's printing shop.

Chapter 6

31. Anicius Mantius Severinus Boëthius was a sixth-century statesman and philosopher in Rome. He befriended King Theodoric of the West Goths but the king eventually had him imprisoned and put to death on suspicions of sins as diverse as republicanism and magic. B. translated and commented on Aristotle. He wrote "On the Consolation of Philosophy," much cherished reading throughout the Middle Ages. The book is not positively Christian but B., having been killed by a heretical (Arian) king, soon became honored as a saint under the name of Saint Severinus. The Boethius passage in question can be found in the work on philosophy's comfort. It says that all humans are endowed with a desire for the true good, for true happiness, "but error leads them astray to false gods . . . and a specious happiness is apprehended in them" (James J. Buchanan, ed., *Boethius: The Consolation of Philosophy* [New York: Frederik Ungar Publishing Co., 1957], Book 3, Prose 2, 3, pp. 23–24). On Boethius, see further Max Manitius, *Geschichte der lateinischen Literatur des Mittelalters* (Munich: C. H. Beck'sche Verlagsbuchh, 1911), vol. 1, pp. 22–36.

32. When the Frankfurter speaks of the "external" he has in mind the good as it appears in the created world and when he speaks of the "internal" he thinks of the good beyond the manifest creation. He deals with the first kind of good in Chapter 55 and with the second kind in Chapter 56.

33. Meister Eckhart uses an image much like this one. He says: "The soul that wishes to find God must leap beyond all creatures" (Pfeiffer, p. 141, 31–32; see Intro., fn. 9).

Chapter 7

34. Eckhart writes: "The Masters say that the soul has two faces. The higher one always sees God, the lower one looks downward and informs the senses. The higher one is the summit of the soul, it gazes into eternity. It knows nothing about time and body." This insight reveals "the origin of the Good ... like a fire ... that is nothing but the Holy Spirit" (Pfeiffer, p. 59, 4–10).

35. The term *created* has immediate reference to life on earth, Christ's earthly existence. *Th. G.* thinks about God as being incarnated in human form through Christ. The word created should therefore be taken to mean "manifested in finite form."

36. Mandel comments: "According to the Christology of *Th. G.*, which described Christ's divinity in keeping with an ethical ideal, i.e., as simply determined by God ... , it was impossible to think of Christ's life as being forsaken by God." "The need for redemption was missing in [medieval] Germanic theology" (p. 17, fn. 1). There is an element of truth in this observation by Mandel. Germanic mysticism placed more emphasis on the "*in* you" than the "*for* you" when it spoke of Christ, the presence rather than the eschaton. But "perfection" in *Th. G.* connotes more than ethical completeness. It means "wholeness," an integration of feeling, thinking, and willing.

37. Würzburg adds two sentences. Their absence in Luther's edition is probably significant. "Therefore, he who desires the one, must relinquish the other. For no one can serve two masters." The statements create difficulty, not least because the reference to Jesus' words about God and Mammon are totally out of place in this context. We have assumed all along that the Luther edition was closer to the original thinking and closer to Luther's thinking.

Chapter 8

38. Würzburg: ... *dahin kommen* ... , "come to this," which is less graphic than Luther's edition: *Dahin lugen ad' sehen.*

39. *Lautter:* the word means "pure" but it is in spiritual parlance a purity arrived at through chastening, a right reading of life's teaching, not the result of mental techniques.

40. *Bilden,* "images." *Th. G.* is here saying what mystical theology has always said. Encounters with eternal life involve a decreasing

reliance on three kinds of images: sensate impressions, pictures of holy imagination, and doctrinal notions.

41. The reference is to Dionysius the Areopagite, the "Pseudo-Dionysius" (sixth century) who influenced Gothic mysticism. Luther had serious questions about Dionysian mysticism. To Luther it tasted too much of self-salvation. In Nathan Söderblom's terminology it was rather a Christianly less acceptable "infinity mysticism" than a Gospel-oriented "personality mysticism" (see Hoffman, *Luther . . .* , pp. 120, 160).

42. Pseudo-Dionysius wrote, among other books, "On the Mystical Theology." In it he mentions "friend Timothy," the addressee of this description of God-union.

43. The Luther edition here lacks some lines found in the Würzburg edition. The Würzburg passage states that the seemingly "impossible" can by perseverance become "quite light and easy." One may experience the Eternal by putting "all strength and energy into it" (Würzburg-Bernhart, p. 104).

44. The *edler Blick*, the "noble glance," of the German original no doubt refers to medieval mystical theology's distinction between the "evening knowledge" about the divine (*cognitio vespertina*) and the "morning knowledge" (*cognitio matutina*). The latter is described as the "nobler."

45. Again, Würzburg here carries a further explication that is missing in the Luther edition. The additional passage could well be interpreted as a description of the effects of prayerful contemplation, in an evangelical sense. But it could also be construed as a proposal for self-development in a manner inimical to the Reformation emphasis on "grace alone." Its absence in the Luther edition is therefore most interesting. Did the Reformer edit the piece out, or—and this is more likely—was it never a part of the Frankfurter's thinking? Turn yourself in spirit to God, says the passage in question, "with your whole heart and mind," and you will experience "a real union." "The truest and the fullest union" may thus be brought about "in this present time." "The kingdom of heaven and eternal life on earth" have been found (Würzburg-Bernhart, p. 104).

Chapter 9
46. A few added lines in Würzburg serve to explicate the statement by repeating that such a posture is due to total dependence on "senses and reason" and the prerequisite for a better state of being is to understand who one is as a person (Würzburg-Bernhart, p. 105).

47. Luther's edition lacks the following explication found in the Würzburg edition: "For sins and wickedness can never make us evil so long as they are outside us, that is, so long as we do not commit or give consent to them" (Würzburg-Bernhart, p. 105).

48. In the Middle Ages much devotion and preaching was focused on the departed saints. Stories about saints were extremely popular reading. The Frankfurter subjects this phenomenon to a mild critique. With Martin Luther this critique grew in intensity.

49. In Würzburg we find a few additional lines at this point that are obviously designed as further explication. The passage states that self-knowledge is the highest "art," higher than well-assimilated information about the planets and stars of the heavens, the plants, the organization of mankind, etc. It concludes, surprisingly, by assigning the wise injunction "Know thyself" to a biblical clairaudient experience. The biblical opinion about self-knowledge would rather be that God knows me but I am hard put to fully know myself (Würzburg-Bernhart, p. 105).

50. See *Das Büchlein vom vollkommenen Leben. Eine deutsche Theologie*, ed. Herrmann Büttner (Jena, 1907). On p. 485 Meister Eckhart is credited with the nucleus of this idea. Eckhart: "Now no going-out can be so noble that the remaining-within would not be nobler." Büttner also finds similarities with Suso (pp. 186 and 235): '. . . the innermost flowing-out toward God." See also Würzburg-Bernhart, p. 201, fn. 25. To traditional theological thought the experience approximating this one is probably the mystery of "incessant praying," treated, for instance, in the Eastern Orthodox *The Way of a Pilgrim*. "Remaining-within," *ynne bleiben*, expresses, according to Mandel (p. 20, fn. 4), a will-oriented view, in contrast to "the official Catholic theology," which spoke of "tasting" and "emotion" rather than of "mobilization of will" and "a carrying out of duties."

51. The Würzburg edition provides a version that renders the statement unintelligible: "Und soll anders der Mensch   immer selig werden . . . so . . . muss das Eine allein in der Seele sein." If the suggestion is that salvation might take place "under different circumstances," it becomes nonsensical to say that it can only happen under *one* circumstance (Würzburg-Bernhart, pp. 105–106).

52. The eternal comes through to us in falling cadences or as the outermost rings in the water after a stone has broken its surface. Meister Eckhart had an extreme expression for this. He said that it is just as inappropriate to express God's reality as "goodness" or "good" as it is to term the sun black (Büttner, p. 78).

53. The One and the Good are coterminous in scholastic theology. See Thomas Aquinas, *Summa Theologiae I:11.* (New York: Blackfriars & McGraw-Hill, 1964), p. 167.

Chapter 10

54. "The true Light" is a term that returns in the present book (see chap. 40). It describes the inner balance that God can bring about from the ground of the soul. Luther often uses the adjective *true* in order to depict that inner awareness of divine resources which implies liberation from captivity in the world of "the false light" (see Hoffman, *Luther . . .*, pp. 51, 149). The false light is selfish, impulse-ridden existence. Suso speaks along this line about new, true light and false light (see *Heinrich Seuse, Deutsche Schriften*, ed. Karl Bihlmeyer [Stuttgart: W. Kohlhammer, 1907; reprint Frankfurt a. M.: Minerva, 1961], pp. 115, 157, 169, 196, 242, 254, 438, 466, 471–472).

55. It should be noted that this statement does not follow the line of "spiritual formation" found in much scholasticism and in some forms of mysticism (cf. Hoffman, *Luther . . .*, pp. 119–122). The traditional idea is that man should by right action strive for the highest Good. *Th. G.* reverses that teaching and says do not strive but surrender.

56. The latter part of this Chapter is slightly larger in the Würzburg edition than in Luther's edition. Man's waywardness receives more attention. But Würzburg carries no essential material over and above the document that Luther sent to the printer in 1518. Würzburg (Würzburg-Bernhart, p. 108) submits explanatory additions that speak of a tension between "spirit and nature." *Th. G.* is closer to Luther's view according to which the real theological tension is between "God and the human self."

Chapter 11

57. The reader can think of two biblical references at this point: 1 Pet. 3:18–19 ("For Christ also died for sins once for all, the righteous for the unrighteous, that he might bring us to God, being put to death in the flesh but made alive in the spirit; in which he went and preached to the spirits in prison") or Mt. 27:46 ("Jesus cried . . . , My God, my God, why hast thou forsaken me?"). I prefer the first one, since it brings out the element of redemption in Christ's deed, Christ as a *sacramentum* in addition to his role as an *exemplum*. Mandel, who generally argues that the element of redemption, the "for you" of Christ's deed, is missing in *Th. G.*, remarks that it is not "absolutely

necessary" to think of "descended into hell" at this point (p. 25, fn. 1)
See also Hoffman, *Luther* . . . , pp. 120, 135.

58. We see here *Th. G.*'s view of the background to "perfection"
or, as I have sometimes translated it, "wholeness": it is not based on a
technique of moral or religious improvement but on grace flowing
into man's heart when he sees his sinfulness.

59. *Meister Eckhart, Vom Zorn der Seele,* ed. H. Büttner, I: 181.

60. I cannot share Mandel's (p. 27, fn. 1) concern about *Th. G.*'s
forgiveness theology in this passage. It seems to me that precisely the
experience of guilt, contrition, and the will's opposition to God, as
here depicted, leads to the experience of forgiveness and abundant
grace, equally graphically described.

61. The Luther edition of *Th. G.*: "Wa die helle vergeet das hy-
melreich besteet" (chap. 15, second page, line 5 in the original; Mandel, p. 27, line 10).

62. Jn. 3:8.

Chapter 12

63. Würzburg adds as an explication: "For the prophet declares,
'There is no peace, says my God, for the wicked.'" (Is. 48:22 and
57:21; Würzburg-Bernhart, p. 111).

64. Jn. 14:27.

65. Würzburg omits the words "all chosen friends of God." It is
possible that a concrete historical fact constitutes the basis here: the
spiritual renewal movement represented by the Friends of God, a
loosely knit fraternity for prayer and piety. Johann Tauler was a
prominent leader among the Friends of God (Würzburg-Bernhart, p.
112).

66. Several expansions of the text in this chapter appear in
Würzburg. The deceitful offers of the world are described as "prom-
ising much and keeping little." The life of man is also depicted as never being free of "troubles and crosses." The peace of salvation is
called a transformer of "the bitter" to "the sweet" and a guarantor of
everlasting peace.

Chapter 12 of the Würzburg edition ends here. The Luther edition has a longer twelfth chapter. We shall follow the Luther edition.
The chapter numberings of the Würzburg edition and the Luther edition part company at this point, as the material has been divided differently.

67. Martin Luther was evidently under the impression, in 1516,
when he first had an (abbreviated) edition of the *Th. G.* published,

that Johann Tauler was the author. In the manuscript used for the present translation it is quite clear that Tauler was not the author. Luther had noted the fact by this time, two years later. We see this in his preface and in the older brief introduction to the book, of anonymous origin.

In prevailing Luther interpretations the Reformer is described as antimystical in the sense that his thought had nothing essential in common with any forms of mysticism. This is a fateful generalization. If, for instance, as Tauler says in the quotation given here, the mystical mode included understanding for the meaningfulness of the "outward sign," Luther had no objection. This insight was part and parcel of Luther's own.

Luther's marginal comment in Latin at this point ("antequam discernant inter figuram et rem figure . . .") implies that he misunderstood the text. He took "the truth" to be the object instead of the subject of the sentence (see Mandel, p. 30).

68. Mystical theology speaks of three moments in the order of salvation: *via purgativa*, the purifying stage; *via illuminativa*, the inner dawning of spiritual truth; and *via unitiva*, the union with God. The Würzburg edition carries a further explication of the Tauler dictum (contained in a separate chapter): "Some people . . . hanker for a flight to heaven." But we are called "to take up our cross and follow Christ" and receive "example, experience, wise counsel and teaching from devout and perfect servants of God." Then follows, in the Würzburg edition, yet another, separate chapter that describes the threefold way to salvation, an elaboration of the points with which Chapter 12 in the Luther edition ends. The "union" is for persons made whole and in that sense "perfect." The heart becomes pure by dint of reliance on God alone, filled with love, enraptured by the vision of God (Würzburg-Bernhart, pp. 113–114).

Chapter 13

69. The Frankfurter does not, on the other hand, think that "the Self" does not contain Godward inclinations. Cf. in the present Chapter the words, "Man is created to true obedience." See also Chapter 26 about the distinction between the "inner man" and the "outer man." The Frankfurter, Tauler, and Luther all reckoned with kinship between God and man, in the sense of a uniting link through the "image of God." Their theological-anthropological postures were such that Jesus' words about the prodigal son in Lk. 15:17 could be interpreted as a word about this linkage: "He came to himself." See Hoffman, *Luther . . .* , Chapter 6.

NOTES

70. Probably an allusion Jn. 1:14: "... the Word became flesh and dwelt among us" and to Eph. 2:21–22: "Christ Jesus ... in whom the whole structure ... grows into a holy temple in the Lord, in whom you also are built into it for a dwelling place of God in the Spirit."

71. Cf. Phil. 2:5–7: "... Christ Jesus, who, though he was in the form of God, did not count equality with God a thing to be grasped, but emptied himself. ..."

72. The Würzburg edition's "explicatory" intent is evidenced by the following addition: "... in other words, God himself, who can do all things."

Chapter 14

73. The standing terms are *selbheyt* and *icheyt*, literally "self-dom" and "I-dom", Luther's "curved in on oneself." But this talk about the dying of the I is not tantamount to "extinction" of self-awareness with mystics like the Frankfurter and Tauler. Some scholarship on Luther claims this, but can do so only with the aid of too wide generalizations (see Hoffman, *Luther...*, pp. 50–51, 145–156).

The Würzburg edition provides some lines of explication. To "die unto himself" means to die to "earthly pleasures, consolations, joys, appetitites. ..." Man "clings" to these but he has to relinquish them if he is to come to the truth (Würzburg-Bernhart, pp. 116–117).

74. The paraphrase may refer to Col. 3:9–10: "... you have put off the old nature with its practices and have put on the new nature, which is being renewed in knowledge after the image of its creator." Or it refers to Eph. 4:22–23: "Put off your old nature which belongs to your former manner of life ... and put on the new nature, created after the likeness of God in true righteousness and holiness." If the reference is to the latter we must of course not place too much emphasis on the suggestion that Saint Paul wrote the whole epistle.

75. Jn. 3:3: "... unless one is born anew, he cannot see the kingdom of God."

76. Matthew 12:30. The previous quotation 1 Cor. 15:22.

77. In its teaching about sin, medieval theology employed the terms *aversio a Deo* and *conversio ad creaturam*, a turning away from God, an "aversion" to Him, and a turning toward the created world, a "conversion" to the world. See Chapters 2 and 4 in the present book to which the Frankfurter obviously refers.

78. Luther uses the expression "one cake with Christ" in order to describe the union between man and God, without, however,

thereby maintaining that our kind of human existence can turn into sinlessness *coram Deo,* before God.

79. *Th. G.*'s way of dealing with "grace," here and in other passages, refutes the notion (with Mandel, for instance) that "perfection," "wholeness," is exclusively ethical in Germanic mysticism.

80. In all likelihood this has reference to 1 Jn. 1:8: "If we say we have no sin, we deceive ourselves, and the truth is not within us."

81. As already pointed out, the Luther edition of *Th. G.* uses the terms *selbheit*/(*selbheyt*) and *icheyt,* which, in a pinch, we could translate as "selfdom," "self-seeking," "selfishness," "I-dom," "I-attachment." However, such words may hide more than they want to reveal. The virtue of using them would lie in the need to make it clear that the Frankfurter is not suggesting an "obliteration" of man's "I"—as many interpreters of Luther and his relationship to medieval theology keep on insisting in their endeavors to remove mystical theology from Luther's essential theological concerns. Rather, the Frankfurter (and, for that matter, Luther and Tauler) speaks of a lower self that becomes wholly identified with the objective world and a higher self that is the "image" of God and the self Jesus refers to in his parable about the prodigal son who finally "came to himself." I refer again to my interpretation of "I-consciousness" in Luther's theology (Hoffman, *Luther* . . . , pp. 51–52, 145–146).

82. This little exception is not found in the Würzburg edition (Bernhart, p. 119).

83. Mandel (p. 36, fn. 3) writes that *Th. G.* here is actually saying that natural man experiences the pain of suffering as a suffering directed against himself whereas God-directed man experiences suffering in such a manner that it makes him want to help remove disobedience in others. But, of course, he cannot achieve this since everyone must do his own penance.

84. *Vergottet* is the term in Luther's edition (as well as in the Würzburg). We have already suggested that a word less objectionable to traditional Christian theology may be "sanctified." However, Luther was not averse to a description of God's work in man very close to the adjective *vergottet.* He certainly did not mind it when he published *Theologia Germanica.* Faith, he said, "is the creator of divinity . . . in us." And in another context he said: "In justification by faith you are shown the right way . . . so that your life . . . becomes wholly divine." See Hoffman, *Luther* . . . , pp. 163–165. S. Winkworth suggests the translation "a partaker of the divine nature" instead of "divinized." The wording can be found in 2 Pet. 1:4. Winkworth, p. 55, see Intro fn. 42.

Chapter 15

85. Würzburg adds: ". . . wanting to be unblemished and innocent, as our first parents Adam and Eve, when they were still in paradise where the one put the blame on the other. He has no right to do this for it is written: 'There is none without sin' (1 Jn. 1:8)" (Würzburg-Bernhart, p. 120).

Chapter 16

86. The humanistic libertinistic movement called the Brothers and Sisters of the Free Spirit may be the target of this reference to a lawless life. Note that the lawless life is lawless because it is not life in God. The ethical and the mystical always interweave. See the Introduction to the present book.

87. Luther's edition here, as in other contexts, uses terms that seem to be closer to divinatory imagination than the Würzburg edition. The knowledge concerning Christ is described as a discovery of *das war einfeltig gut*, "the true goodness that is harmlessness" or "single-mindedness," "guilelessness." *Einfeltig* means "childishly trusting," "single-minded," or both in combination. "Harmless" is another good interpretation; we have it in connection with Jesus' words about the spiritual-psychological result of a life in God: "harmless as doves" (Mt. 10:16). The term *einfeltig* depicts an attitude to fellow beings that is free from barbs because it is single-mindedly resting in God. The "goodness" about which the Frankfurter speaks is therefore not primarily obedience to a set of moral rules but the outflow of a divine justification experience. Würzburg has the following version of the same passage: ". . . das wahre einige Gut." This version presents the mystery of Christ's life in philosophical rather than religious terms: "the true, sole good." It describes a state rather than a relation (Würzburg-Bernhart, p. 121).

88. 1 Cor. 13:10: "When the perfect comes, the imperfect will pass away."

Chapter 17

89. The reference to "natural reasoning" is found in the Luther edition, not in Würzburg (Würzburg-Bernhart, p. 123). Mandel (p. 39, fn. 4) says that "Hunnius took umbrage at *Th. G.* but Arndt praised it" on account of this passage. Aegidius Hunnius was an orthodox Lutheran professor in the sixteenth century. Johann Arndt, 1555-1621, pastor and bishop, exerted great influence through his widely read books on a devout life. See *Johann Arndt, True Christianity*, trans. and intro. by Peter Erb (New York: Paulist Press, 1979).

90. The reader is reminded that the Frankfurter's anthropology contains a dual view of the self: the lower self and the higher self. Apparently with Luther's theological approval he refers to the lower self as self-aggrandizement, barring the way to "the perfect Good."

91. The first part of the paraphrased Bible quotation comes from Mt. 16:24: "If any man would come after me, let him deny himself and take up his cross and follow me." The second part alludes to Mt. 10:37–38: "He who loves father or mother more than me is not worthy of me . . . and he who does not take his cross and follow me is not worthy of me."

Chapter 19

92. Würzburg submits the opposite suggestion: "er hätte wohl bisweilen weniger zu beschicken," (less action) rather than the Luther edition's "er het etwan mehr zu schicken" (more action). It would seem that the former version supports the general, erroneous notion that all mysticism is passive in relation to moral responsibility. It would therefore be more reasonable to suppose that the version Luther submitted to the Wittenberg printer in 1518 is the more acceptable one, and in keeping with Luther's dynamic view of the intimate relationship between the mystical and the moral.

Chapter 20

93. Both the Luther edition and the Würzburg edition use the word *besessen*, for which the nearest English equivalent is "possessed." However, the text suggests a distinction between a temporary "obsession" (*besessen*) and a more lasting hold on the victim, "possession," (*behafft*), which signifies a more outdrawn "ownership" of the human vehicle. Accordingly, we shall make this distinction here between being obsessed by the devil and possessed by him.

94. The first part of this quotation refers to Rom. 8:14: "For all who are led by the Spirit of God are sons of God." The latter part comes from Rom. 6:14: "For sin will have no dominion over you, since you are not under law but under grace."

95. Mt. 10:20.

96. The Brothers and Sisters of the Free Spirit are, as in similar allusions in *Th. G.*, probably the object of this declaration. Free will, they said, does not exist except by divine fiat, a sort of transfusion of will, a deterministic way of dealing with good and evil. Mandel (p. 43, fn. 5) finds that *Th. G.* goes to the other extreme: Salvation depends on man's effort. I think that Mandel overemphasizes *Th. G.*'s activism.

NOTES

97. Here John the Baptist comes to mind. He "prepared" the way before the Lord (Mt. 11:10). He also enjoined to repentance as preparation: "Repent for the kingdom of heaven is at hand. For this is he who was spoken of by the prophet Isaiah when he said: '... Prepare the way of the Lord, make his paths straight'" (Mt. 3:2–3).

98. Saint Paul's words about the dialectic and paradoxicalness of the religious life are brought to mind: "... work out your own salvation with fear and trembling; for God is at work in you, both to will and to work for his good pleasure" (Phil. 2:12–13).

99. Tauler says in a sermon (*Johannes Tauler, Predigten*, trans. and ed. Walter Lehmann, 2 vols., [Jena, 1913], 1, 18ff.) that God himself prepares the ground in man, i.e., frees the soul for man's new birth and his new work.

100. Jesus pointed out that "he who seeks will find" (Mt. 7.8). The concern that this talk about "preparation" is Pelagianism appears unfounded, seen in the context of the entire book.

Chapter 21

101. *Gelassen*, (a.) and *gelassenheit* (n.) are words that elude the English language. *Gelassen* has something in it of the Latin *non calere* and the French derivation "nonchalant," etymologically meaning "not heated up." There is an element of "detachment from vicissitudes" in the word. But it is a detachment engendered by religious devotion, not by philosophical speculation. "Calm," "freedom from care and anxiety," "serenity," are other possible translations. "Serene" and "serenity" have been chosen here.

102. Devotion to the divine must, in other words, lead to a full participation in incarnate existence. If we are to use the word *mysticism* for *Th. G.*'s way of describing life in God, it is ethical rather than abstract mysticism.

103. Lk. 23:34.

104. Würzburg-Bernhart adds (p. 128): "... may he strive after it unwearingly and perseveringly. Then he will doubtless come to the eternal end. 'For he that endures to the end will be saved'" (Mt. 10:22).

Chapter 22

105. Both Würzburg and the Luther edition present material here that, inexplicably, rightly belongs to the Chapter numbered 20 in the Luther edition and 22 in Würzburg.

106. Cf. Gal. 2:20: "... it is no longer I who live, but Christ who

lives in me"; and Eph. 4:24: ". . . and put on the new nature created after the likeness of God in true righteousness and holiness." The ethical ideal is God's presence in man as a total being.

107. The more intimate man's life in God is, the more sensitive it becomes to that which detracts from God.

108. It is worth repeating that the Frankfurter actually writes *selbheyt* and *icheit*, which are rendered "self" and "I" in this translation. It should be pointed out again that *Th. G.* does not speak of obliteration of that "I" or "self" which is the ground of our being but rather the lower self, which is molded exclusively by the impressions and the values of the objective world.

Chapter 23

109. No doubt the Frankfurter here thinks of the Brothers and Sisters of the Free Spirit (see the Introduction of the present book).

Chapter 24

110. *Armut*. The word, used several times in this Chapter, expresses what Phil. 2:7 says about Christ: ". . . he emptied himself, taking the form of a servant." The translation, "poverty," should be interpreted against this background.

111. The Frankfurter here expounds a theme Jesus touched on in answer to the disciples' question about greatness. "Truly I say to you, unless you turn and become like children, you will never enter the kingdom of heaven. Whoever humbles himself like this child, he is the greatest in the kingdom of heaven" (Mt. 18:3–4). Luther, who saw the close connection between life in God and life in the world, wrote that the Christian life consists of "obedience and humble submission to all creatures for God's sake" (*W* 1; 263, 16).

112. This, taken superficially, may sound like socio-ethical quietism. However, it must be remembered that *Th. G.* uses this language about the right *religious* posture of man. It certainly does not draw the conclusion that "rights" should be no concern in our *moral* life, expecially if it is a matter of the neighbor's needs.

113. As at the very end of Chapter 17, *Th. G.* here uses *blindheit* as a term for ego-centered existence. Egotism is blindness to the objective fact, namely our involution in self. Luther likewise emphasized that law causes us to discover grace and in that way become "seeing."

114. Mt. 11:29.

115. The term is *die ee*, basically "marital union," in a derived

sense, "covenant." Bridal metaphor, frequently applied by Luther, is common in mystical writings; however, it is not much in evidence with the Frankfurter.

116. Würzburg here adds: "He says" 'I have come not to break covenant and law but to fulfill them' " (Würzburg-Bernhart, p. 135). Cf. Mt. 5:17: "Think not that I have come to abolish the law and the prophets; I have come not to abolish them but to fulfill them." "The law" is, as in the passage, treated in the previous footnote, rendered *die ee* in *Th. G.*

117. Würzburg quotes Jesus in support of the last sentence: "Unless your righteousness exceeds that of the scribes and the Pharisees, you will never enter the kingdom of heaven" (Mt. 5:20). The subsequent comment in Würzburg deals with Christ's emphasis on evil thoughts, not only evil deeds, and suggests that the law allows for temporal goods, yet one should "scorn" them, on Christ's counsel. The law permits vengeance, yet Christ enjoins us to love. But "Christ taught nothing that he did not keep in his life" (Würzburg-Bernhart, p. 135).

118. The reference might be Rom. 11:27: ". . . this will be my covenant with them when I take away their sins"; or 1 Cor. 11:25: ". . . this cup is the new covenant in my blood"; or Gal. 4:4–5: ". . . God sent forth his Son to redeem those who were under the law."

119. Mt. 20:28.

120. *Armut*. See this Chap., fn. 110.

121. Martin Luther wrote in the margin of the 1516 edition of *Th. G.* a word of explication: "Ubi deus est nostrum ego et tota intentio" ("where God is our self and our entire desire") (Mandel, p. 51, fn. 6).

122. Mt. 26:38. Here Würzburg interjects in explanatory fashion: During his earthly life "he did not have one good day, but only sadness, suffering and adversity. Therefore the same should occur with his servant, too."

123. Mt. 5:3.

124. This counterpoint piece is found in the Luther edition but not in the Würzburg edition.

125. This sentence is a little awkward in the context for the next sentence begins with a "but."

126. Mandel, p. 52, places inside this sentence these words: ". . . und diss was yn Christo." They belong more properly to the subsequent sentence and have been so translated here.

NOTES

Chapter 25

127. In the original of the 1518 Wittenberg edition, used for the present translation, this Chapter is erroneously numbered XXIX.

128. Mt. 19:21: "Jesus said to him: 'If you would be perfect, go, sell what you possess. . . .'" The movement of the Free Spirit is the target here. Within it one said that perfection included no sustained attention to ordinary duties.

Chapter 27

129. This was an assertion made by the Brothers and Sisters of the Free Spirit.

130. Mt. 26:32; Mk. 14:28. The last part of the quotation is from Mt. 28:7 or Mk. 16:7.

131. Lk. 24:39.

Chapter 28

132. Würzburg's *fur nichts achten*, "consider as nought," does not fit the context as readily as the Luther edition's *uñ v'nichtē*, "and destroy," "do away with."

133. Rom. 8:14: "For all who are led by the Spirit of God are sons of God," and 6:14: "For sin will have no dominion over you, since you are not under law but under grace."

134. The ethic expounded here is not teleological. The Frankfurter grounds the moral life in a personal disposition. He describes teleological morality as legalism, as too heavy a dependence on law. The freedom of a Christian person is anchored precisely in that union with God which engenders freedom, which then proves to contain order.

Chapter 29

135. The original copy of 1518, used for the present translation, erroneously numbers this Chapter 25. It is obviously a question of a typesetting mistake in that the numbers for Chapter 25 and Chapter 29 have been mistakenly exchanged for each other.

136. The Free Spirits in the days of the Frankfurter considered the "Christ life" as a lower level life, containing the obligation to keep external rules.

137. *Lumen increatum*, uncreated light, and *lumen creatum*, created light, are the two technical terms used for the two aspects of God here discussed by the Frankfurter. One can also speak of uncreated grace, describing God, and created grace, temporal revelation, incarnation, grace as it appears in man.

NOTES

138. The scholastic language made a distinction between *divinitas* and *deus*. *Divinitas*, the Godhead, is the ineffable force beyond all empirical manifestations. *Deus* is manifested divinity, eminently present in the Trinity. Meister Eckhart called the two aspects *gotheit* ("Godhead") and *got* ("God"). Luther distinguished in this tradition between God as *increatus* and *creatus*, God as *nudus* and God as *revelatus*.

139. God, says the Frankfurter, assumes His full reality in a conscious, will-imbued being. When he speaks of differentiation between "persons" here, he has at least introduced the second person of the Trinity, the Word. Although several scholars deny that *Th. G.* has a theology of the Trinity because it has no room for the Holy Spirit (f.i. Mandel, p. 58, fn. 2), I find that the entire treatment of sanctification or "divinization" in this book implies the presence of the Spirit.

140. Traditional theological thought speaks of "God's free, creative activity." The creation of the world would then be referred to "God's free decision." The Frankfurter is closer to Neoplatonism in that he considers "God-as-God" as of necessity manifesting Himself in the created order. But he is also close to incarnational theology when he says that God without creation is "useless." However, the notion of the inevitability and necessity of the world as an outflow of God does, from a logical point of view, war against the traditional "church dogma." The traditional church dogma speaks of the freedom of God's creative activity. If God is perfect, the creation of the world should be his sovereign and free choice (see Würzburg-Bernhart's comments, p. 206, fn. 73).

141. Those who object on theological grounds to the Frankfurter's linkage of God's "destiny" to that of the created world should pay attention to these words. He knows that he has been in deep water, yet he reminds us here that God's "investment" in the created world is so intimate and so necessary that the question of divine "meaning" ought to include the illogical one: Would God not be God without the world? It is almost like asking the philosophical question: Does that forest exist which you have never seen?

Chapter 30

142. Thomas Aquinas speaks of "a supernatural God-knowledge." That is to say, from man's point of view, we share in God by recognizing God, interiorly, through the natural light of our reason. The gift of the light of grace flows into and strengthens the natural light. Man acknowledges God when God makes Himself known to man. This is of course a statement that does not satisfy the theory of

knowledge and the anthropology presupposed by much Protestant theological thinking. The latter rejects Thomas Aquinas's supposition, in evidence here, that the natural light of reason is strengthened by the inpouring of divine light by grace (Würzburg-Bernhart, p. 206, fn. 74). However, Lutheran theologies (among other Protestant theologies) have been so adamant in their epistemological rampart building that they have found it impossible to integrate with their Luther interpretation precisely the supernatural elements in Luther's thinking about faith and his anthropological assumptions about God's inner space in man. The inner space is always, says Luther, that "knowledge of God" which "is divinely imprinted upon all men's minds" (Hoffman, *Luther . . .* , p. 138; *WT* 5; 368).

143. See the last fn. to Chapter 29 about the theologically illogical idea that the omnipotent Being should need a created world.

144. Würzburg-Bernhart does not contain "I love you." (Bernhart, p. 146).

145. *Th. G.* is not saying that God has to be subsumed under Goodness. God is essentially the one Good. From that point of view God lacks "I-dom." He does not step out of "the Good" in order to have something for Himself (Cf. Mandel, p. 61 fn. 1).

146. The reader is reminded that the original uses the terms *icheit* and *selbheit*, which do convey better than the translation's "I" and "self" that we are not dealing with an obliteration of man's self but rather with a reduction to nothingness of "I-dom" and "self-dom," the self-centered ego of our temporal existence, "the lower self."

Chapter 31

147. A new, *personal* relationship has emerged. It is governed by love. It has melted down the natural, ice-cold intent to seek vengeance. This love submits no conditions, since its ultimate ground is the unconditional Good, within which the claims of the ego are like chaff in the wind.

148. Mt. 26:50: "Friend, why are you here?"

149. Lk. 23:34. Anselm's redemption theory seems to be indirectly rejected here. Divine love excludes the possibility that God would demand punishment for sin or satisfaction for it through Christ. Yet, *Th. G.* reckons with God's "wrath" in the following way: Human self-will clashes with God's will; Christ's abandonment and His death become not a means to satisfy an objective criminal code but rather the removal of God's wrath relationship to man; this removal can occur only by man's entering into the very abandonment and death experi-

ence initiated by Christ and a corollary recognition of the basis for God's "wrath" (self-will clashing with God's will). See Mandel, pp. 63–63, fn. 3.

150. Jn. 18:11: "Put your sword into its sheath; shall I not drink the cup which the Father has given me?"

Chapter 32

151. Würzburg adds: "For in hell self-will is the best fuel. That is why one says: Give up your own self-will and there will be no hell" (Würzburg-Bernhart, p. 148).

152. Würzburg adds: ". . . in anything, be it spiritual or natural, but only the praise and honor of God and His divine will" (Würzburg-Bernhart, p. 149).

153. Würzburg adds: ". . . and surrenders his own will and only brings out God's will" (Würzburg-Bernhart, p. 149).

154. Mt. 10:39: "He who finds his life will lose it, and he who loses his life for my sake will find it." Mk. 8:35: "For whoever would save his life will lose it; and whoever loses his life for my sake and the Gospel's will save it." Lk. 9:24: "For whoever would save his life will lose it; and whoever loses his life for my sake, he will save it." *RSV* uses the word *life* for the original's *die seel*. In the present translation, "soul" is preferred, since it is the choice of *Th. G.*

Chapter 33

155. Herein lies the beginning of all ethics.

156. Mt. 5:3.

Chapter 34

157. "Being" is here explained in terms that prevent the tendency of some mysticism to call matter and creation "bad" or "anti-God" and only the invisible and spiritual "good" and "of God."

158. Mt. 12:30.

Chapter 35

159. We see again that the Frankfurter shies away from the idea that God's relationship to sin is that of the judge, dispensing justice on the basis of the law book of objective justice. Rather, the propitiation is God's personal involvement.

Chapter 36

160. Mt. 11:30 might be the background here: Jesus says: "My yoke is easy, and my burden is light."

Chapter 37

161. The word we have translated into "rectitude," namely *redlicheit*, may also mean "sincerity," "integrity." Rectitude seems to fit the context best here and at other points where *redlicheit* appears as part of lists of virtues pertaining to right living (Chapters 26 and 28).

162. Previously, especially in Chapter 29, we have been acquainted with the Frankfurter's distinction between "God as Godhead" and "God as God." Here this distinction reappears with special reference to the structured moral life of a Christ follower, a manifestation of "God as God."

163. "... wurd sein etwan v'saumt on geuerd uñ der gleich. ... " Würzburg provides the unlikely version: "... und wurde von ungefähr etwas versäumt ... ," ("... if something were approximately neglected ...") (Würzburg-Bernhart, p. 70).

164. Obviously a reference to the Brothers and Sisters of the Free Spirit, a movement that drew adherents from disparate quarters in medieval times. Common to them all was their antichurch bias. As stated earlier, the movement had its roots in thirteenth-century philosophies of Neoplatonic bent and in Waldes's and Francis's poverty ideal. It represented a spiritualism that Luther rejected. As we see here and elsewhere, it was also rejected by *Th. G.*

165. They maintain a posture between the ruleless indifference of the Free Spirits and the anxious concern of those who are moral out of a desire for reward.

Chapter 38

166. The reader is again reminded that the German original speaks of *icheit* and *selbheit* (not with consistency in spelling), words that should literally be translated "I-dom" and "selfdom." However, awkwardness prevents such a rendition. It should be remembered that, when a divinized person forsakes "I" and "self," the reference is to the lower self. The implied "obliteration" of I and self does not include the higher self, which in salvation by grace is reminded of its origin. It is important to keep this in mind since much theological critique of mysticism assumes that all mystics speak in favor of complete obliteration of the self or the I, as already pointed out in other contexts.

167. Is. 14:13–14: "You said in your heart, 'I will ascend to heaven; above the stars of God I will set my throne on high ... I will ascend above the heights of the clouds, I will make myself like the most high.'"

168. "... auff sich selber gekert...." Cf. Luther's term "curved in on the self."

169. Würzburg derives amplifications from Jn. 12:25 rendered as follows: "He who loves his soul loses it." (As noted above, *RSV* translates "life" where the Frankfurter uses "soul.") Würzburg comments: "All the goodness, aid, comfort and joy which are in the creature, in heaven or on earth, a true lover of God finds comprehended in God himself" (Würzburg-Bernhart, p. 161). Würzburg then enlarges on this theme (Würzburg-Bernhart, pp. 161–162).

170. *Th. G.* uses the term *gewissen* in a sense that exceeds the meaning of "conscience." It is therefore sometimes preferable to render *gewissen* as "knowledge of sin," "awareness of sin," or "sin-consciousness."

171. Again, the term is *gewissen*, "conscience." However, it would lead us astray to say that Christ lacked conscience.

172. Whenever *die natur* is used by the Frankfurter it must not be interpreted in the limited sense of sensate experience. It includes everything that has to do with the Pauline *sarx*, "flesh," which includes man's emotional body. It is important to keep this in mind since the popular standard interpretation of mysticism operates with the idea that "nature" in mystical parlance *always* implies a Platonic division between matter and spirit, resolvable only by flight from matter. "Incarnation theology" is marshaled against "mystical theology." This tenacious standard objection against "Greek philosophy" almost prohibits a just treatment of Luther's use of mystics and of the term *mystical*.

Chapter 39

173. Throughout this translation the Frankfurter's word *vergotten* has been rendered "divinized." The term *divinized* often meets with inner resistance on the part of those who consider the evangelical faith almost the opposite of divinization, man being considered, theologically speaking, totally depraved. The term *divinized* is not much different from the word *sanctified*. In that regard *Th. G.* merits Luther's confidence also with respect to Christian anthropology. See Luther's way of dealing with divinization in Hoffman, *Luther...*, pp. 138, 164–165. This particular passage provides us with two terms for the same thing, *vergotten* and *gotlich*; the latter could, in my judgment, also be rendered "sanctified." S. Winkworth translates *gotlich* either "godlike" or "divine" (Winkworth, p. 146).

174. *Untugent*.

175. *Tugentsaz,* "virtuous." The Frankfurter speaks here of the true nature of morality. We should keep this in mind lest the old-fashioned words "virtue" and "virtuous" might peradventure make us miss the implication. The implication is that the moral life is rooted in life-in-God and basically never related to outward success.

176. *Untugentsam,* "unvirtuous," "immoral."

177. *Gerechtickeit* and *ungerechtickeit* are the words used by the Frankfurter. They could be translated as "justice," "injustice," or "righteousness," "unrighteousness." If the reader would feel that "justice-injustice" better expresses the sociomoral content, he or she is welcome to read that connotation into my rendering, "righteousness-unrighteousness." For the sociomoral component is definitely there.

178. We are reminded of Jesus' words: "He who is not with me is against me and he that does not gather with me scatters" (Mt. 12:30). There is, according to *Th. G.*—and its approving editor, Martin Luther—no neutrality for those who have been touched by the kingdom.

179. This is no literal quotation. Closest to the dictum comes a verse in Is. 5 rather than 6. We cite Is. 5:20: "Woe to those who call evil good and good evil, who put darkness for light and light for darkness, who put bitter for sweet and sweet for bitter."

Chapter 40

180. As though catechetical or theological information would generate knowledge of God. Much medieval mystical theology was opposed to some forms of scholasticism on this score. Theological interpretations of Luther's thought have often, erroneously, assumed that his rejection of scholastic rationalism automatically included a rejection of mystical theology (see Hoffman, *Luther . . .* , pp. 133–134).

181. Würzburg suggests *menschen* instead of the Luther edition's *personen* (Würzburg-Bernhart, p. 166). The latter is preferable. The context is after all the distinction between human incarnation and divine glory.

Chapter 41

182. As we have already observed, the Frankfurter, like other medieval mystics, does not speak in terms of "obliteration of the I." He rather speaks of the surrender of self-ishness. Many assessments of medieval mysticism erroneously assume that *all* mystical theologies espouse the ideas of "infinity mysticism." No concession is given to the thought that a good many Christian mystics are adherents to

"personality mysticism." (The terms are Nathan Söderblom's.) Mandel suggests that the expression "das ist gottes eigen . . . on alsvil tzu der personlicheit gehört" in effect says that it is God's characteristic to be void of I-claims, except that He loves Himself as the perfect Good (Mandel, p. 82. fn. 1.). The present translator sides with Bernhart, p. 171, and Winkworth, p. 159. Both assume, basing their translations on Würzburg, that the Frankfurter means that we cannot be so totally free from concern for self that we are unable to exist on the incarnated plane of personality.

183. Mt. 11:30: "For my yoke is easy, and my burden is light."

184. The Frankfurter deals with "nature" as the natural inclination of man to curve everything in on himself. He thinks the same way as Luther about man's situation. This is pointed out here on account of the common theological tendency to read into every suggestion that "nature must be conquered" an unevangelical, "Greek" philosophy.

185. "Aus dissem vorgesprochen mag man noch neher versten uñ bekennē dan hie kein unterscheid ist." Mandel places "dan . . . ist" within parentheses (p. 85). Bernhart, using Würzburg, has the following version: "Therefore, from the above one can understand and discern more than is expounded here" (p. 173). Winkworth follows the Würzburg version: "From what hath here been said, ye may understand and perceive more than hath been expressly set forth" (p. 165).

Chapter 42

186. Mt. 12:30: "He who is not with me is against me, and he who does not gather with me scatters."

187. Cf. Jesus' words: "I do not seek my own glory" (Jn. 8:50), and Paul's words: "Let no one seek his own good" (1 Cor. 10:24); ". . . not seeking my own advantage" (1 Cor. 10:33).

188. This theme no doubt appealed to Martin Luther, who had found merit-seeking for God's favor an occupation that actually militated against the Gospel.

Chapter 43

189. ". . . wer an Christum gelaubet, der glaubet das seyn leben. . . ." *Gelauben* or *glauben* does not mean merely embracing a verity with your intellect but an inward "knowing."

190. Note the close connection between life in God and life in the world, the mystical and the ethical.

191. Gal. 2:20: "It is no longer I who live but Christ who lives in me."

Chapter 44

192. From the aspect of life in this world God is a "Nothing." But He is at the same time *in* everything and everyone as their being and life.

193. The Luther edition has *icht*, which actually means "anything." Würzburg has *etwas*, "something" (Bernhart, p. 176).

194. "... wil oder mag got nit geleiden." Würzburg, in Bernhart's ed., p. 177, renders the passage as follows: "... will und kann Gott nicht erleiden." S. Winkworth translates: "... is truly fighting against God." Winkworth's previous translation of *Gott erleiden* is "be still under God." The latter is preferable. The context seems to require the translation offered here (Winkworth, p. 174).

Chapter 45

195. Luther gave expression to the same thought when, in a table conversation, he said about God's immanence everywhere: "As God can be housed in the virgin's womb, He can also be housed in the creature." Someone asked him: "Would God consequently be in the devil?" "Yes, certainly in substance even in hell ... as Psalm 139 says: 'If I make my bed in sheol, thou art there.' " See Hoffman, Luther ..., pp. 142–143, *WT* 1; 101, 27–37.

196. The theory of knowledge underlying much Western theology is founded on an anthropology that looks askance at a suggestion like this one by *Th. G.* However, the idea that man is "continuous" with God through his religious impulse coincides with much scriptural evidence (f.i. Lk. 15:27) and spiritual experience. Mystical theology takes for granted that, since God created the world, the world has its "essence" in God more truly than in itself. The "ground of being" in man is that "image" of God in man which is stirred by the impact of God's love and grace.

197. We find in theological comments on statements like these about a dimension of "being" beyond this world a constant concern about "Platonic thought," influencing Christianity with thoughts of "a metaphysical world." On Christian territory, God as Creator is the fountainhead for our determinate existence. Augustine and the mystics whom Luther cherished said similar things about the supernatural source that creates and informs our world. Although not ideal and much abused, the adjective *supernatural* will have to be reinstated in

theological vocabulary. It should be done, however, on the understanding that the deepest in the "natural" is allied with the "supernatural."

Chapter 46

198. Mk. 16:16: "He who believes and is baptized will be saved; but he who does not believe will be condemned."

199. This brings to mind Luther's treatment of "historical faith" and "inner faith." They belong closely together, he said. The devil recognizes historical faith but shies away at inner faith. See Hoffman, *Luther . . .* , pp. 149–150.

Chapter 47

200. The Free Spirit people (see the Introduction) claimed that hell is man's own will and breaking one's self-will is to break hell. In other words, they rejected the notion that hell is a reality that exceeds and exists beyond the empirical world. *Th. G.*, of course, combats this humanistic supposition.

201. Lk. 10:18: "And he said to them, 'I saw Satan fall like lightning from heaven.' "

202. The appreciation of the created order that permeates the Frankfurter's book is a constant refutation of the allegation that all mysticism is Platonic in the sense that it always denigrates the sensate, life in matter and body.

203. The allusion here is to Gen. 2:15–17: "The Lord God took the man and put him in the garden of Eden to till it and keep it. And the Lord God commanded the man, saying: 'You may freely eat of every tree of the garden; but of the tree of the knowledge of good and evil you shall not eat. . . .' " Moreover, the total approach to Creation in *Th. G.* reminds us of Gen. 1:31: "And God saw everything that he had made, and behold, it was very good."

Chapter 49

204. This sentence is missing in Würzburg (Bernhart, p. 183). Instead, the subsequent sentence is repeated.

Chapter 50

205. *Th. G.* speaks of freedom from self-will. All empirical bindings should be abandoned. It is not a matter of Christian ethical heteronomy but rather a Christian ethics where freedom is a "freedom for

God." Luther called the will, thus liberated, *voluntas nuda*, "the naked will" (Mandel, pp. 94–95, fn. 6).

206. Jn. 8:32, 36.

Chapter 52

207. Luther saw his theology as a "cross theology" from this angle, especially in earlier years. That is to say, surrender of self is cross. Later he also combined the teaching about the cross with a more objective theory of redemption.

208. Mt. 10:38: "And he who does not take his cross and follow me is not worthy of me." Lk. 14:27: "Whoever does not bear his own cross and come after me cannot be my disciple." About "leaving all" the Frankfurter might have had Mt. 19:27 in mind: "Then Peter said in reply, 'Lo, we have left everything and followed you. . . . '"

209. Jn. 14:6: "Jesus said to him, 'I am the way, and the truth, and the life; no one comes to the Father but by me."

210. Winkworth: ". . . follower of Christ more truly than we can understand or set forth" (p. 197).

Chapter 53

211. Jn. 12:26.

212. Jn. 17:24: "Father, I desire that they also, whom thou hast given me, may be with me where I am."

213. Jn. 10:1–3: "Truly, truly, I say to you, he who does not enter the sheepfold by the door but climbs in by another way, that man is a thief and a robber; but he who enters by the door is the shepherd of the sheep. To him the gatekeeper opens. . . . "

214. The word here is *unachtsamkeit:* "inattention," "sloppiness," "slovenliness."

215. Jn. 6:44: "No one can come to me unless the Father who sent me draws him."

216. Würzburg suggests the following version: ". . . so muss es [das wahre Gut] auch in allem sein. . . . " The Luther edition says: ". . . so muss es [das war gut] auch allein sein." The present translation prefers the version of the Luther edition, since it agrees better with the context to say *allein, in et per se,* than *in allem,* "in all." Winkworth (p. 200) uses *in allem* here and ten lines later *allein,* rendering it "the Only One." Würzburg has *in allem* in both places.

217. Mandel (p. 99) takes the liberty of putting editorial quotation marks around *nit* in his rendition of *Th. G.* The suggestion is that

nit should be considered a noun, meaning "nought." There is no such indication in the Luther edition of the Wittenberg 1518 print, which served as basis for the present translation. Hence "Darum nennet man es auch nit" has been rendered: ". . . therefore has no name." One sentence later the use of *ungenant* as a word for the ineffable serves as a confirmation of this translation. Bernhart also, and erroneously, it seems, uses *nichts*, "nought," in his Würzburg edition (p. 190) whereas Winkworth has "cannot be named" (p. 200).

Chapter 54
218. Jn. 14:6.
219. Jn. 6:44.
220. 1 Cor. 13:10.

Chapter 56
221. Cf. 1 Cor 2:9: "What no eye has seen, nor ear heard, nor the heart of man conceived, what God has prepared for those who love him. . . . "
222. Würzburg adds: "It hinders man on his way to the perfect life; he will never attain it unless he leaves everything, first of all himself. For no one can serve two masters, who oppose one another. If you want the one, you have to leave the other. Therefore: if the Creator is to take over, all creatures must get out. Know this" (Würzburg-Bernhart, p. 193).
223. Würzburg expatiates on this, the central injunction being "that the soul and the body with all its members be so willing and prepared for that to which God has created them . . ." (Würzburg-Bernhart, p. 194).
224. Würzburg expands: ". . . all creatures are subject to man, serving him, so that man may be subject to God and serve Him" (Würzburg-Bernhart, p. 194).
225. Jn. 10:1: "Truly, truly I say to you, he who does not enter the sheepfold by the door but climbs in by another way, that man is a thief and a robber." In Würzburg the paraphrase on Jn. 10:1 is followed by an explication of what "thief" and "murderer" mean. "Thieving," in the context, is interpreted as "robbing God of his glory." "Murdering" means that "he murders his own soul" and "all who follow him, by his doctrine and example." The section ends with a word about "humble obedience" (Würzburg-Bernhart, p. 195).
226. Würzburg has the following ending in Bernhart's edition:

NOTES

". . . may he help us who surrendered his will to his heavenly Father,
Jesus Christ, our dear Lord who is exalted over all things in eternity.
Amen" (Würzburg-Bernhart, p. 196). Winkworth's translation offers
a third version: ". . . Jesus Christ our Lord to whom be blessing for
ever and ever. Amen" (p. 213).

Bibliography

Books

Arndt, Johann. *True Christianity.* Trans. and intro. Peter Erb. New York: Paulist Press, 1979.

Asheim, Ivar (ed.). *The Church, Mysticism, Sanctification and the Natural in Luther's Thought.* Philadelphia: Fortress, 1967.

Baring, Georg. *Bibliographie der Ausgaben der "Theologia Deutsch", 1516–1961, Ein Beitrag zur Lutherbiographie.* Baden-Baden: Verlag Heitz, 1963.

Barth, Karl. *Church Dogmatics.* Vols. I–IV. Edingburgh: T. & T. Clark, 1960–1969.

Benzing, Joseph. *Lutherbibliographie.* Baden-Baden: Verlag Librarie Heitz, 1966.

Bernhart, Joseph. (trans. & ed.) *Der Frankfurter, eine deutsche Theologie.* Leipzig: Im Insel-Verlag, 1920.

Blakney, Raymond Bernard (trans.). *Meister Eckhart, A Modern Translation.* New York: Harper & Brothers, 1941.

Boethius, Anicius M. S. *The Consolation of Philosophy.* Trans. James J. Buchanan. New York: Frederik Ungar Publishing Co., 1957.

Büttner, Herrmann (ed.). *Das Büchlein vom vollkommenen Leben.Eine deutsche Theologie.* Jena: 1907.

Büttner, Hermann. (trans. & ed.). *Meister Eckeharts Schriften und Predigten.* Jena: Eugen Diederichs, 1921.

Clark, James & Skinner, John V. (trans. & eds.). *Meister Eckhart, Selected Treatises and Sermons.* London: Faber & Faber, 1958.

Clark, James M. *The Great German Mystics.* Oxford: Basil Blackwell, 1949.

BIBLIOGRAPHY

Evans, C. de B. (trans.). *Meister Eckhart by Franz Pfeiffer.* New York: Lucis Publishing Co., n.d.

Filthaut, E. (ed.). *Johannes Tauler, Ein deutscher Mystiker.* Essen: Driever Verlag, 1961.

Hägglund, Bengt. *The Background of Luther's Doctrine of Justification in Late Medieval Theology.* Philadelphia: Fortress, 1971.

Harnack, Adolf. *History of Dogma.* Vols. I–VIII. 3rd ed. London: Williams and Norgate, 1896–1899.

Hofmann, Georg (ed.) *Johannes Taulers Predigten.* Freiburg: Herder, 1961.

Hoffman, Bengt R. *Luther and the Mystics.* Minneapolis: Augsburg, 1976.

Holmquist, Hjalmar. *Kyrkohistoria.* Vols. I–III. 2nd ed. Stockholm: P.A. Norstedt & Söner, 1928–1931.

Kepler, Thomas S. (trans.). *Theologia Germanica. The Way to a Sinless Life.* Cleveland & New York: World Publishing Co., 1952, 1961(?).

Lehmann, Walter. (trans. & ed.) *Johannes Tauler: Predigten,* Vols. I–II. Jena: 1913.

Luther, Martin. *D. Martin Luthers Werke,* Kritische Gesamtausgabe. Weimar: Böhlaus (1883–   ) _____, Briefwechsel. Weimar: Böhlaus, 1930–1970, _____, Tischreden Weimar: Böhlaus, 1912–1921.

———*Luther's Works.* Vols I–LIV. Eds. H. T. Lehmann and J. Pelikan. St. Louis and Philadelphia: Fortress and Concordia, 1955–1967.

Malcolm Mrs. (trans). *Old German Theology. A Hundred Years Before the Reformation.* London: Arthur Hall, Virtue & Co., 1854.

Mandel, Hermann (ed.) *Theologia Deutsch* , vol. 7 in *Quellenschriften zur Geschichte des Protestantismus,* eds. Joh. Kunze and C. Stange. Leipzig: A. Deichert'sche Verlagsbuchh. Nachf. Georg Boehme, 1906.

Manitius, Max. *Geschichte der lateinischen Literatur des Mittelalters.* Munich: C. H. Beck'sche Verlagsbuchh., 1911.

Neander, August. *General History of the Christian Religion and Church.* Vols. I–V. Boston: Crocker & Brewster, 1859.

Nielsen Fredrik (ed.). *Kirke-leksikon for Norden.* Vols. I–IV. Aarhus: Albert Bayers Forlag, 1900–1929.

Pfeiffer, Franz (ed.). *Deutsche Mystiker des vierzehnten Jahrhunderts.* Leipzig, 1857; Scientia Verlag Aalen, 1962.

Ritschl, Albrecht. *Geschichte des Pietismus in der reformierten Kirche.* Vols. I–III. Bonn: Adolph Marcus, 1880–1886.

Seuse, Heinrich. *Deutsche Schriften.* Ed. Karl Bihlmeyer. Stuttgart: W. Kohlhammer, 1907; reprint Frankfurt a.M.: Minerva, 1961.

BIBLIOGRAPHY

Skinner, John V., see Clark, James.

Söderblom, Nathan. *Till mystikens helysning.* Ed. Hans Åkerberg. Lund: Studentlitteratur, 1975.

Steiner, Rudolf, *Mysticism at the Dawn of the Modern Age.* Trans. Karl E. Zimmer. Englewood, N.J.: Rudolf Steiner Publications, 1960.

Thomas Aquinas. *Summa Theologiae.* New York: Blackfriars & McGraw-Hill, 1964.

Uhl, Willo. *Der Franckforter ("Eyn deutsch Theologia").* Bonn: Marcus & Weber, 1912.

The Way of a Pilgrim. Trans. R. M. French, 2nd ed. New York: Harper and Brothers, 1952.

Winkworth, Susanna (trans.). *The History and Life of the Reverend Doctor John Tauler of Strasbourg.* New York: Wiley & Halsted, 1858.

Winkworth, Susanna (trans.) *Theologia Germanica.* London: Macmillan & Co., 1874.

Articles

Baring, Georg. "Neues von der 'Theologia Deutsch' und ihrer weltweiten Bedeutung", *Archiv der Reformationsgeschichte,* vol 48, 1957.

Hoffman, Bengt R. "On the Relationship between Mystical Faith and Moral Life in Luther's Thought," *Bulletin, Lutheran Theological Seminary at Gettysburg,* vol. 55:1, February 1975.

———. "Luther and the Mystical," *The Lutheran Quarterly,* vol. 26:3, August 1974.

Oberman, Heiko. "Simul gemitus et raptus: Luther und die Mystik," Asheim, Ivar, ed., *The Church, Mysticism, Sanctification and the Natural in Luther's Thought.* Philadelphia: Fortress, 1967.

Index to Preface, Foreword, Introduction and Notes

Concupiscence, 162.
Confession, 4.
Conscience, 22, 183.
Constance, 10.
Contemplation, 6, 7, 26, 166.
Contrition, display of, 5; doctrine of,
  xii; for sin, xi–xii, 169; and Spirit,
  xiii.
Conversion, xii, 10, 17, 18, 28.
1 Corinthians, 1, 42; 1:17, 157; 2:9, 189;
  10:24, 185; 10:33, 185; 11:25, 177;
  13:10, 158, 159, 173, 189; 15:22, 171.
2 Corinthians, 3:5, 164; 10:10, 157.
Covenant, 19, 177.
Creation, xi; and deism, 163; and God,
  22, 179; goodness of, 35; of man, 50,
  170; and necessity, 21, 179, 180; of
  self, 36.
Cross, 19; bearing of, 22, 37, 40, 169,
  170, 174, 188; of Christ, 19, 22.
Crusades, 2.
Damnation, 22.
David of Dinant, 21.
Deism, 163.
Denck, 25.
Denifle, 11.
Dessau, 156.
Devil, xvi, 22, 48, 162, 174, 186, 187.
Dionysius, Pseudo-, 166.
Disciples, xiii.
Doctrine, xii.
Dominicans, 4, 7, 9, 10, 42, 155.
Dualism, 31, 34, 163.
Ebner, Christina, 8, 9.
Ebner, Margareta, 8, 9.
Eckhart, 8, 14–19, 32, 153, 163–165,
  167, 179.
Egotism, 26, 176, 180.
Engeltal, 8, 9.
Enlightenment, age of, 24.
Enthusiasts, 21, 25, 28, 31.
Ephesians, 2:21–22, 171; 4:22–23, 171;
  4:24, 176.
Epistemology, 180.
Erb, Peter, 173.
Erdmann, J. E., 32.
Erfurt, 43.
Ethics, cosmological, 162; Christian, 34,
  37, 39, 40, 165, 187; and dualism, 31,
  34; and Free Spirits, xvi, 23, 173, 182;
  grounding of, 34–41, 181; and life in
  God, 23; and mysticism, 173, 174,
  175, 185; and responsibility, 36, 37,
  39–41; of second mile, 37–38;

teleological, 178; and *Theologia
  Germanica*, 34–41, 162.
Evans, C. de B., 153.
Eve, 173.
Evil, 5, 184.
Excommunication, 3, 4.
Existence, incarnated, 34, 175; ordinary,
  36.
Experience, cf. also *Sapientia
  experimentalis*; and contrition, xi; of
  forgiveness, 169; of God's love, 36; of
  God's presence, 158, 161; of Lord's
  presence, 40.
Faith, Christian, xiii, xiv, 20; creates
  divinity in man, 159, 172; doctrine
  of, xii, 180; evangelical, 25, 183;
  historical, 187; inner, 187; and
  justification, 158, 172; life of, 27; and
  morality, 40; purification of, 6; as
  sapientia experimentalis, 161; and
  truth, xiii.
Farel, Guillaume, 26.
Father, 6, 41, 181, 188, 190.
Fear, 6, 7.
Filthaut, E., 152, 153.
Flacius, Mathias, 27.
Formula of Concord, 27.
Francis, 182.
Franciscans, 4.
Franck, Sebastian, 25, 26.
Frankfurt am Main, 2, 26, 151.
Frankfurter, 49, 151, 159; anthropology
  of, 170, 174; ethics of, 31, 35–41, 162,
  173, 178, 184; and Free Spirits, 21,
  176, 178; and Friends of God, 17; and
  Luther, 170, 172, 177, 185; and
  mysticism, 9, 171, 177, 187; and
  Tauler, 17, 19, 20, 170, 171, 172;
  theology of, 50, 160–164, 166, 167,
  170–173, 176, 178, 179, 181–185.
Fredrick of Austria, 2–3.
Fredrick II, 5.
Free Spirits, see under Brothers and
  Sisters of the Free Spirit.
Friends of God, 6–8, 158; and clergy, 4,
  7, 9, 25; and Free Spirits, 7, 21; and
  inner way, 8; and Luther, 20; and
  mysticism, 33; and renewal, 6; and
  Tauler, 10, 17, 18, 169; teachings of,
  7; and *Theologia Germanica*, xvi, 7, 9,
  14, 17, 169; theology of, 17, 19;
  writings of, 13.
Galatians, 2:20, 175, 186; 4:4–5, 177.
Genesis, 1:27, 50; 1:31, 187; 2:15–17, 187.

197

Knights of St. John, 11.
Knowledge, and Christ, 173;
experiential, 20, 36; and God, 17, 18,
167, 179, 180, 184; of Good, xii; of
Lord, 39; of self, xii, 167; of sin, 183;
theory of, 186; of world, 163.
Königsberg, 151.
Kunze, Joh., 154.
Last Day, 5.
Law, xii, 38, 39, 174, 177, 178, 181.
"Layman from Oberwald", 11.
Lehmann, H. T., 154.
Lehmann, Walter, 175.
Leipzig, 43, 44.
Libertinism, 7, 23, 173.
Life, cf. also Christ; Christ-, xvi, 16, 28;
Christian, xii, xiv, 25, 26, 176, 181;
eternal, 6, 165, 166; in God, 1, 16, 23,
35, 40, 41, 173, 175, 176, 184, 185;
godly, 32; of good, xii, 182; inner, 29;
modes of, xi, xiii, xiv; moral, xvi,
xvii, 33, 35, 36, 37, 38, 40, 176, 178,
182, 184; new, xiii, and order, 39;
renewal of, xvi, 40; in the Spirit, 18;
spiritual, xii, xvi, 7, 23; uncertainties
of, 7, 20, 169; in world, 41, 176, 185,
186.
Light, Christ, 28; created, 178; false,
xiii, 168; and morality, 38; in spirit,
19; true, xiii, 39, 168; uncreated, 178.
Lisco, F. G., 32.
Lord, 6, 40, 171.
Louis of Bavaria, 3–4.
Love, cf. also God; false, xiii; ground
of, 180; for all men, 40, 180; true, xii,
xiii, 39.
Lucifer, xiii.
Luke, 9:24, 181; 10:18, 187; 14:27, 188;
15:17, 170; 15:27, 186; 23:34, 175, 180;
24:39, 178.
Luther, Martin, 21, 24, 167; Christology
of, 16; and ethics, 36–41; and
Frankfurter, 170, 172, 177, 185; and
Friends of God, 20; and justification,
7, 14, 153, 163; and mysticism, xvi, 9,
14, 16, 33, 153, 158, 166, 170, 174, 177,
182, 183, 186; and Tauler, xvi, 20, 41,
42, 44, 154, 155, 170; and *Theologia
Germanica*, xiv, xv, xvi, 1, 2, 9, 13–15,
17, 20, 24–25, 27–32, 34, 151, 158,
177, 183; theology of, xii, 7, 15, 16,
20, 28, 32, 158, 163, 168, 172, 174, 176,
179, 180, 184, 185, 188.
Lutherans, and Enthusiasts, 28; and

mysticism, 25, 30; orthodoxy, 28, 29,
30, 159; and pietism, 29, 30; and
Theologia Germanica, 25, 27, 28, 29,
30; theology of, 180.
Malcolm, Mrs., 156.
Mammon, 165.
Man, cf. also Union; as little Christs,
163; conversion of, xii, 17; as curved
in on himself, 36, 171, 183, 185;
destination of, xi, xii, 175;
divinization of, xvi, 16, 17, 40, 159,
172, 182, 183; existence of, 17;
faculties of, 15; God in, 15, 153, 164,
180; and God, xi–xiii, xvi, 2, 6, 12,
15, 16, 19, 20, 24, 35, 158, 159, 163,
168, 170, 179, 180, 186, 189; from
God, 15; -in-God, 16; ground of, 16;
as image of God, 170, 171, 172, 176,
186; inner, 170; kinship with God,
19; is led by God, 18, 178; natural,
31; and neighbor, xii; new, xiii, 26,
175; old, xiii, 27; outer-, 170;
restoration of, xiii; sinfulness of, 15,
20, 162, 169, 183; supernatural, 31.
Mandel, Hermann, 46, 48, 49, 154, 155,
156, 157, 159, 160, 161, 162, 163, 165,
167, 168, 169, 170, 172, 173, 174, 177,
179, 180, 181, 185, 188.
Manitius, Max, 164.
Maria-Medingen, 8, 9.
Mark, 8:35, 181; 16:16, 187.
Martyrs, 12.
Mass, and Interdict, 4.
Matter, 181, 183, 187.
Matthew, 3:2–3, 175; 5:3, 177, 181; 5:17,
177; 5:20, 177; 7:8, 175; 10:6, 173;
10:20, 174; 10:22, 175; 10:37–38, 174;
10:39, 181; 11:10, 175; 11:29, 176;
11:30, 181, 185; 12:30, 171, 181, 184,
185; 14:28, 178; 16:7, 178; 16:24, xiii;
17, xiii; 18:3–4, 176; 19:21, 178; 19:27,
188; 20:28, 177; 26:32, 178; 26:38, 177;
26:50, 180; 27:46, 168; 28:7, 178.
Meisterbuch, 11.
Melanchthon, 27.
Mercy, 5.
Merit, 185.
Merswin, Rulmann, 10–12.
Morality, cf. also Ethics; 36, 184; and
Free Spirits, 22–23, 38, 182.
Mysticism, cf. also Luther, Tauler;
Christian, xiv, 166, 184; and church,
1; and ethics, 173, 174, 175, 185;
Germanic, 158, 165, 172; infinity-, 20,

198

185; curved in on, 36, 171, 183, 185;
-denial, xii, xiii, 6, 31, 174;
extinguished, 36, 171, 176, 180, 182,
184, 188; freeing from, 32, 168; and
God, 35; is God, 22; higher-, 172, 174,
182; lower-, xii, 17, 172, 174, 176, 180,
182; -knowledge, xii; -salvation, 166;
and sin, 24, 32; unworthiness of, xii;
-will, xvi, 16, 22, 35, 36, 38, 153.
Selnecker, Nicolaus, 27.
Serenity, 24, 28, 175.
Servet, Miguel, 27.
Severinus, cf. under Boethius.
Siedel, Gottlob, 48.
Sin, 27, 33, 48; and Christ, 168, 177,
180–181; and condemnation, xii; as
contrary to God, 35, 169, 171, 180,
181; contrition for, xi–xii; and God,
181; liberated from, 174, 178; mortal,
23; original, 28; and punishment,
180; and satisfaction for, 180; and
will, 162, 180.
Skinner, John V., 152, 153.
Söderblom, Nathan, 20, 153, 166, 185.
Son, 177.
Soul, changed, 35–36; and Christ, xvi,
162; dark night of, 16; essence of, 19;
faces of, 165; God in, 19, 20; ground
of, 19, 20, 164, 168; prepares for God,
15, 17, 161, 165, 175, 189; and
quietism, 163, 164; rest of, 34;
surrender of, 36; as temple, 15.
Spalatin, 41, 154.
Spener, Philip Jakob, 30, 32.
Spirituality, 6, 29, 163.
Stange, C., 154.
Staupitz, Johann, 24.
Strasbourg, 4, 7, 9, 10, 18.
Steiner, Rudolf, 153.
Supernatural, 186–187.
Suso, Heinrich, 9, 10, 167, 168.
Tauler, Johann, 5, 11, 30, 49, 50; and
Eckhart, 14–20, 32; and Frankfurter,
17, 19, 20, 170, 171, 172; and Free
Spirits, 23; and Friends of God, 10,
12, 17, 18, 169; and Luther, xvi, 20,
41, 42, 44, 154, 155, 170; and
mysticism, xvi, 9, 14, 16, 153; and
Theologia Germanica, 13, 14, 24, 28,
41, 42, 44, 47, 155, 170; theology of,
19, 154, 172, 175.
Templars, French, 6.
Teutonic Order, 2.
Theodoric, 164.

Theologia Germanica, cf. also the
Frankfurter; 5; authorship of, xi, xv,
xvi, 1–2, 8, 9, 12, 17, 41, 42, 44, 151,
155, 158, 170; banned, 13; and ethics,
34–41, 162; and Free Spirits, 7, 12,
21, 24, 173, 174, 182, 187; and Friends
of God, xvi, 9, 14, 17, 169; God
"speaks the book", 1, 8, 151; Large
Theologia, 43, 44, 45, 47, 151, 155;
and Luther, xiv, xv, xvi, 1, 2, 9,
13–15, 17, 20, 24–25, 27–32, 34, 158,
177, 183; and Luther's Preface, 1, 2,
42; manuscripts of, xv, 1, 34, 41–48,
152, 156, 157; and mysticism, xiv,
14–20, 24, 29, 34, 37, 158, 175, 177,
183, 184; and Protestants, 24–34;
Small Theologia, 2, 43, 44, 151, 155;
sources of, 44, 46; style of, xiv, 1, 31,
42, 50; and Tauler, 13, 14, 24, 28, 41,
42, 44, 47, 155, 170; title of, 41, 43,
44, 45; translations of, xv, xvi, 13, 14,
25, 26, 32, 44–50, 156, 178, 181, 183,
185, 186, 189.
Theologia Germanica, Editions of, xiv,
xv, xvi, 13–15, 24, 29, 31, 32, 34,
41–49, 154, 158; of Augsburg, 44; of
Büttner, 157; of Luther, xiv, xv, xvi,
1, 2, 13–15, 32, 34, 41–49, 152, 155,
157, 159–170, 172–175, 177, 178, 184,
186, 188, 189; of Mandel, 49;
Würzburg, 13, 14, 34, 45–49, 152,
155–157, 160–162, 164–175, 177, 181,
183–186, 188, 189; Würzburg-
Bernhart, 152, 154, 156, 157, 160, 161,
166, 167, 169–173, 175, 177, 179–184,
187, 189, 190.
Theology, cf. also Mysticism; biblical,
32; evangelical, 158; and Free Spirits,
22; German, 158, 165; "heart", 30;
incarnational, 183; negative, 160;
Protestant, 33, 180; Reformed, 26, 27,
30; Roman, 29, 31, 167; and *sapientia
experimentalis,* 34; and sin, 171; and
spirituality, 13; traditional, 13, 21,
167, 172, 179; Western, 14, 33, 186.
Thomas Aquinas, 12, 18, 162, 163, 168,
179, 180.
Transcendence, 33.
Trinity, 41, 179.
Troxler, 31.
True Christianity, 30, 173.
Truth, xiii, 18, 171.
Uhl, Willo, 155, 156.
Union, in Body of Christ, xvi; through

201

Index to Text

203

CARDINAL BERAN LIBRARY
ST. MARY'S SEMINARY

3 3747 00040 9349

DATE DUE

54743

Der Franckforter.
The Theologia Germanica of
Martin Luther

BV
4831
.D47

c.3

CARDINAL BERAN LIBRARY
ST. MARY'S SEMINARY
9845 Memorial Drive
Houston, Texas 77024

GAYLORD